why
beckett

ENOCH BRATER

why beckett

with 122 illustrations

THAMES AND HUDSON

For Robert H. Chapman

© 1989 Thames and Hudson Ltd, London

First published in the United States in 1989 by
Thames and Hudson Inc., 500 Fifth Avenue,
New York, New York 10110

Library of Congress Catalog Card Number 88-51346

Printed and bound in the German Democratic Republic

Contents

1 Samuel Beckett, 1973

On a fine sunny morning in the mid-1960s Samuel Beckett was walking to the Lord's Cricket Ground across Regent's Park. He had travelled to London from Paris specially for the test match between England and Australia, staying with the publisher John Calder at his house behind Wigmore Street. John Gibson, an Irish director in the BBC radio department, remembered how enthusiastic the playwright was about the green trees, the birds singing, the company of good friends, the beautiful blue sky. At this someone remarked, "Yes, on a day like this it's good to be alive." To which Beckett replied: "Well, I wouldn't go as far as that!"

This anecdote of Martin Esslin's is revealing, situating us, as it does, somewhere between hope and despair. That is essentially how it is in Beckett's imaginative world. In *Waiting for Godot*, his landmark play, two characters with the script names Vladimir and Estragon (but who in performances call one another Didi and Gogo) anticipate for two acts the arrival of a "kind of acquaintance" who never appears. Their only scenery is a rock, a single tree, and a landscape leading nowhere: "What is there to recognize?" says Gogo. Though they never stop waiting on their lonely country road, their constant vigil in the theater is not without its sometimes somber, sometimes hilarious qualifications. "Nothing is certain," Vladimir demurs to his sidekick, "when you're about." As the dramatic action, or lack of it, unfolds, this weary player will later universalize, "But at this place, at this moment of time, all mankind is us, whether we like it or not." Estragon, taking the measure of the unfortunate Lucky, will be similarly global in his commentary: "He's all humanity."

Beckett used a school notebook to work on *Waiting for Godot* in the late 1940s. He composed in French. Later he rendered *En attendant Godot* into English by himself because, as he said, he felt "bad having to change what someone else had translated." For his novel *Molloy*, also conceived in French, he had engaged Patrick Bowles to carry out the work. In the end, in fairness to the young writer, he decided to do the French-English translation on his own, a strategy he has

2 *Beckett, with his brother Frank in 1954 during his last months at Shottery, Killiney. Frank died that September, survived by his wife Jean (d. 1966) and two children, Edward and Caroline.*

3 *Cooldrinagh, Beckett's childhood home. In the interior of the house the signature of a young "Samuel Beckett" is carved into the mahogany panelling of the hall and stairway.*

4 *William Frank Beckett* (right) *seated next to Fred Clarke, Clerk of the Leopardstown Racecourse, in suburban Foxrock*

5 *Leopardstown Racecourse from Foxrock Railway Station*

generally employed ever since. Beckett began the *Godot* project methodically, writing only on his schoolbook's right hand pages; when he ran out of space, he backed up to the verso sides he had skipped before. Beckett first calls Vladimir "Lévy"; in the second act, he abruptly gives him the name by which he has become known to two generations of theatergoers. Unlike most of his manuscripts, the text for this play was written clearly, almost, it seems, without hesitation. "It wrote itself," he told Peter Lennon, "with very few corrections, in four months." Today the famous notebook (dated "9 October 1948" and "29 January 1949") is housed in a bank vault in Paris, not far from Beckett's apartment on the boulevard Saint-Jacques.

Beckett's journey to the *Godot* country is a little drama of its own, though the author would most likely be reluctant to describe it as such. He was born in 1906 at Cooldrinagh, the spacious family home his father had built at the junction of Kerrymount Avenue and the Brighton Road in Foxrock, an affluent Dublin suburb favored by the Protestant Irish upper middle-class. His parents were May Roe Beckett (1871–1950), serious about churchgoing, hens, donkeys, and dogs, and William Frank Beckett (1871–1933), a civil engineer who had offices at Beckett and Medcalf, 6 Clare Street, Dublin. Samuel Barclay was the younger of their two children; his brother, Frank Edward, born four years earlier, died of lung cancer in 1954. One curiosity surrounding Beckett's birth concerns the uncertainty of the date itself. Though the birth certificate his father filed in the district of Stillorgan, County Dublin, lists May 13 on the registry, Beckett insists that he was born on April 13, 1906—Good Friday as well as Friday the thirteenth.

"You might say I had a happy childhood," Beckett once observed, "although I had little talent for happiness. My parents did everything that could be done to make a child happy. But I was often lonely." His mother was stern and severe in managing the Beckett household. Mary Manning Howe, a childhood friend, remembers her as "a recluse," almost "a nun." She was "a very moody person, very moody . . . I think the boys were rather in awe of her." Born at Roe Hall in Tipperary, she had been a hospital nurse in Dublin before marrying Beckett's father. Bill Beckett was far more "sentimental." He took his boys on long walks in the Foxrock hills and, as they grew, almost "desperately tried to understand" them. Years later Beckett remembered the Dublin country his father loved so much. "If there is a paradise," he wrote in 1955 to Susan Manning, Mary's mother, "father is still striding along in his old clothes with his dog. At night, when I can't sleep, I do the old walks again and stand beside him again one Xmas morning in the fields near Glencullen, listening to the chapel bells. Or, near the end, in the lee of the rocks on the top of Three Rock, rubbing his feet with snow to try and bring back the circulation."

6 *May Beckett*, c. *1947*

7 *The main building of Portora Royal School*

8 Right: *The Examination Hall, Trinity College, Dublin*

Beckett's education was typical of the wealthy sons of the suburban Dublin Protestants. After attending the kindergarten run by the Elsner sisters, two German ladies immortalized for their love of "too much music" in *Molloy*, Beckett joined his brother at the Earlsfort House School near the now demolished Harcourt Street Station in Dublin. Alfred Le Peton, French as well as Professor of French, served as director of the primary school. In 1920 Beckett followed his brother to the Portora Royal School, overlooking Lough Erne in Enniskillen, County Fermanagh, in the province of Ulster, now Northern Ireland. The school had been founded in 1618 by King James I for "the sons of Protestant gentlemen from all parts of Ireland." The name of one such son, Oscar Wilde, was in due course removed from the prize boards, though today, happily, a portrait of the author of *The Importance of Being Earnest* hangs proudly in the school. At Portora Beckett was more celebrated for sports than for scholarship: rugby, swimming,

9 *Beckett, seated right, with the Portora Cricket Team in 1923*

and, of course, the School Cricket XI. "What ruined me at bottom was athletics," he wrote much later, tongue very much in cheek.

In October 1923 Beckett enrolled in Trinity College, Dublin. Though he continued to excel as batsman and bowler on the cricket team, winning a place for himself in Wisden, the annual publication of notable achievements on the field, it was there that his education really began. As an undergraduate Beckett lived in rooms in New Square, overlooking one of the college's sheltered greens. He studied first arts, then modern languages; he read Baudelaire with Thomas Rudmose-Brown and Dante with Walter Starkie. His tutor, A. A. Luce, an editor of Bishop Berkeley's philosophical works, had done his own research on Descartes. Beckett was fully expected to take up an academic career. When he left college in 1927, a prize student, he could look forward to Paris: he had received the coveted appointment as Trinity's prestigious *lecteur d'anglais* at the Ecole Normale Supérieure. The position, however, did not begin until the following October. He spent the nine-month interval teaching French at Campbell College, Belfast, a time he remembers as "grim."

10, 11, 12 Below: *Trinity College, as seen from outside the gates.* Opposite: above, *the Examination Hall, and* below, *the College Library*

Beckett had been to France before. In the summer of 1926 he bicycled through the Loire Valley and made a special trip to the burial place of "the deaf conceited lecherous laypriest" Ronsard at the Prieuré de Saint-Cosme near Tours. "I took a time exposure," he wrote mockingly, "and wept into my hat." Despite the irreverent tone, Beckett's interests by this time had become increasingly literary. The Paris he discovered in 1928–30 represented to this young Irishman a world of possibilities he had only heard about back home. Dada was dead, but the work of the Surrealists and other experimental writers was still being published in the little magazines he could find on the Left Bank. The pocket theaters off the rue Mouffetard were alive with new and often confusing work, and the more avant-garde showrooms were hanging the kind of picture Beckett would not have been likely to see at Dublin's National Gallery. American movies were being discussed, seriously, as "film." Paris was yesterday, but it was very much today for this provincial lecturer from afar. Besides, Paris was where James Joyce was. And one can only imagine what *that* meant to an impressionable Irish academic whose head was full of Dante and symbolist poetry.

It was Thomas McGreevy who first introduced Beckett to James Joyce. McGreevy, ten years Beckett's senior, had preceded him at both Trinity and the Ecole Normale; later he became the director of the National Gallery of Ireland which, until his death in 1967, he helped to establish as a major European

15   Left: *The rooftops of the Ecole Normale Supérieure on the rue d'Ulm in Paris*

16   *Le Théâtre des Noctambules on the rue Champollion under the Occupation*

17   *A Paris "pocket" theater on the rue du Vieux-Colombier in 1960*

18   *Lucia Joyce in 1926*

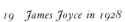

19   *James Joyce in 1928*

20   Right: *Snapshot taken in 1938 by Peggy Guggenheim at Yew Tree Cottage, her country house in Sussex. Seated from left to right are Peggy's daughter Pegeen, George Reavey, Geer van Velde, Gwynned Reavey, Beckett, and Lisl van Velde.*

collection. McGreevy was thus responsible for one of the century's most notable literary relationships, a friendship Beckett was later to memorialize in *Ohio Impromptu*: "Stay where we were once so long alone together, my shade will comfort you." Though it is not true, as frequently claimed, that Beckett was Joyce's official secretary, he did offer help from time to time. Joyce, soon to be legally blind, was relieved to entrust his papers to such capable younger hands. The university-trained Beckett proved to be a valuable resource; on their walks together on the Isle of Swans from the Pont de Grenelle Beckett could hold in check (and sometimes correct) Joyce's penchant for literary misquotation, which was not always intentional. On musical evenings Joyce's son Giorgio sang Schubert while Beckett accompanied him on the piano. Lucia, Joyce's daughter, whose emotional state was already precarious, liked to believe that Beckett came to the apartment to see her, not her father. Beckett felt obliged to tell her otherwise. At the time he was also being pursued by Peggy Guggenheim, the "Mother Pegg" of *Endgame*. In June 1988 Stephen Joyce, Giorgio's son, announced to a stunned audience at the James Joyce Symposium in Venice that he had destroyed three items from Beckett's correspondence to his aunt Lucia: a telegram, a card, and a letter. Before doing so, he asked Beckett what to do with the papers. "Destroy them," he responded. "No one was going to set their eyes on them and repsychoanalyze my poor aunt," Stephen Joyce said. "She went through enough of that when she was alive." Lucia Joyce died in 1982 at St. Andrew's Hospital in Northampton after spending more than 50 years in mental institutions. During the War Beckett had been concerned with getting her to England and out of Nazi-occupied France; he remained a loyal friend to the end.

*21   James Joyce at Sylvia Beach's Paris bookshop, Shakespeare and Company. Beckett's "Dante
. . . Bruno. Vico . . Joyce" was the lead essay in the symposium on* Work in Progress *(Finnegans
Wake) which she published in 1929.*

It was hard to give up the excitement of Paris when the lectureship came to an end. He had to abandon the plans he made with Alfred Péron to translate into French the "Anna Livia Plurabelle" section of *Finnegans Wake*, then called merely *Work in Progress*, though he did complete "Dante . . . Bruno . Vico . . Joyce," where each period in the title stands for a century. The latter became in 1929 the lead essay in a volume Joyce himself entitled *Our Exagmination Round His Factification for Incamination of Work in Progress.* Beckett's piece in *Our Exag*, as the book became known by Sylvia Beach, its publisher at Shakespeare and Company, has been the source of much "literary bookkeeping" by critics of both Irish authors. "His writing," Beckett wrote of Joyce (though it might be equally well said of himself), "is not *about* something; *it is that something itself.*" In Paris Beckett had also written his first published poem, "Whoroscope," which launched Nancy Cunard on her new enterprise at the Hours Press. Advised by Richard Aldington, she had offered a prize for the best work, not to exceed 100 lines, on the subject of time. Beckett, who had been reading Adrien Baillet's life of Descartes, seized the opportunity to compose a witty parody of French philosophy. He walked away with a run of 300 copies as well as the promised ten pounds, but not without a caveat. Nancy Cunard suggested that the author consider adding footnotes to the 98-line text, which, while it reflected accurate information, might only be understood by dedicated Cartesians. Beckett complied. What he presented to the Hours Press, however, was an elaborate send-up of the kind of documentation a modern reader associates with T. S. Eliot in *The Waste Land*. "Eliot hated my work," Beckett said in 1981. "I guess hated is not the word but he disliked my work and made no secret of it."

WHOROSCOPE
SAMUEL BECKETT
An edition of 100 hand-set and printed in 16pt. Caslon Old Face, signed and numbered & bound in scarlet paper
A plaquette   30 f1 Price Five Shillings
And 200 unsigned 6/1 Price One Shilling
    This poem was awarded the Ten Pound Prize for the best poem on Time in the Competition judged by Richard Aldington and Nancy Cunard at the Hours Press. It is Mr. Beckett's first separately published work.

22 *A page from the Hours Press catalogue, 1930, announcing the publication of "Whoroscope" in Paris*

WHOROSCOPE

by

SAMUEL BECKETT

H
O · U
R · T · R
S · H · S
P · E · S
R · E

15, Rue Guénégaud, Paris - 6ᵉ

1930

26.1.59   Ussy-sur-Marne

Bien chère Nancy

Thanks for your letter and the nice things you say about that jolly evening in Sloane Square.

Whoroscope was indeed entered for your competition and the prize of I think 1000 francs. I knew nothing about it till afternoon of last day of entry, wrote first half before dinner, had a guzzle of salad and Chambertin at the Cochon de Lait, went back to the Ecole and finished it about three in the morning. Then walked down to the Rue Guénégaud and put it in your box. That's how it was and them were the days.

I was very disappointed we did not meet in London. I had a brief and exhausting time there trying to get things the way I wanted, right or wrong. I was very pleased with Krapp, but not with Endgame, which needed another week's rehearsal.

You wouldn't know where to live these days, or why. Here is the best I have, not a sound and the Ile de France bowing itself out. I don't find solitude agonising, on the contrary. Holes in paper open and take me fathoms from anywhere.

Much love and vivement les retrouvailles.

Beckett returned to Dublin in 1930 because the terms of his award specified that, on completion of his two years at the Ecole Normale, he would teach at Trinity for another three. The second condition was that he complete his M.A. thesis, which his mentor, Rudmose-Brown, had assumed all along would be on the obscure but academically acceptable subject of Pierre Jouve, a member of the French poetic movement called Unanisme. What he offered in its place came as a complete surprise: a monograph on Marcel Proust. "It is a very youthful work," Beckett would write about *Proust* in 1953, "but perhaps not entirely beside the point. Its premises are less feeble than its conclusions."

26 Left: Jacket cover for the first edition of
Proust, *published in London on March 5, 1931,*
by Chatto and Windus, as the seventh volume
in the Dolphin Book series

28 Below: Jack B. Yeats, The Corner Boys,
c. *1910. The work once belonged to Beckett,*
and is now in the collection of his nephew.

27 Jack B. Yeats, Self-portrait, c. *1920*

Beckett cut an odd figure when he moved next door to the undergraduate
quarters he had occupied in New Square. By this time he had replaced his sensible
Irish tweeds with the tight-fitting French suits he had acquired in Paris. He made
one lasting contact during this period, the painter Jack B. Yeats, the poet's
brother. Years later he would decorate his Paris apartment with a canvas given to
him by the Dublin friend he honored in "Hommage à Jack B. Yeats," a poem
published in *Les Lettres Nouvelles* for April 1954. A translation of Beckett's
tribute, originally written on the occasion of a Paris exhibition of the 84-year-old
artist's work, was included in the catalogue of Yeats's paintings edited by James
White.

Beckett made his only known stage appearance in a short skit he wrote after his return to Trinity with Georges Pelorson, an exchange student from Paris. The revue was called *Le Kid*; the title was a burlesque of Corneille as well as a nod to the popular movie Charlie Chaplin made in 1921 with the child star, Jackie Coogan. Beckett played the part of his own Don Diègue in period costume, but he wore a bowler hat and used an umbrella instead of a sword. *Le Kid* also earned Beckett his first stage review. The college newspaper uncharitably wished Mr. Beckett "would explain his explanations." Here, indeed, a petulant student critic complained, was Trinity's "exhausted aesthete." Undaunted, Beckett completed his treatise on *A la recherche du temps perdu*, paid his fees, and finally obtained his degree in December 1931. But by then he was determined to put an end to his career at Trinity, "this hateful comedy of lecturing." He could no longer bear the absurdity, he wrote from Germany, of teaching to others what he did not fully understand himself. He had decided to become a poet, "the last ditch for an unemployable man."

29 Left: *Charlie Chaplin in* The Kid, *1921. At Trinity Beckett coauthored a "Cornelian nightmare" called* Le Kid, *playing the part of his own Don Diègue when the work was performed at the Peacock Theatre on February 19, 1931.*

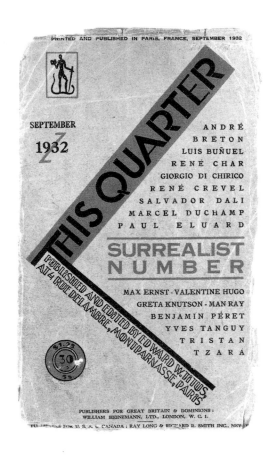

PRINTED AND PUBLISHED IN PARIS, FRANCE, SEPTEMBER 1932

SEPTEMBER 1932

THIS QUARTER

PUBLISHED AND EDITED BY EDWARD W. TITUS AT 4 RUE DELAMBRE, MONTPARNASSE, PARIS

ANDRÉ BRETON
LUIS BUÑUEL
RENÉ CHAR
GIORGIO DI CHIRICO
RENÉ CREVEL
SALVADOR DALI
MARCEL DUCHAMP
PAUL ELUARD

SURREALIST NUMBER

MAX ERNST - VALENTINE HUGO
GRETA KNUTSON - MAN RAY
BENJAMIN PÉRET
YVES TANGUY
TRISTAN TZARA

$1.25 30 5s

PUBLISHERS FOR GREAT BRITAIN & DOMINIONS:
WILLIAM HEINEMANN, LTD., LONDON, W. C. 1.
PUBLISHERS FOR U. S. A. & CANADA: RAY LONG & RICHARD R. SMITH INC., NEW

30 *The cover of the special Surrealist number of* This Quarter *(September 1932), for which Beckett did English translations*

The self-imposed exile was to be only short-lived. From Kassel, where he was visiting the Sinclairs, his Aunt Cissie's family, he travelled south to Paris and moved into the Hotel Trianon on the rue de Vaugirard, where McGreevy was living. He was going to write a novel. But *Dream of Fair to Middling Women* proved recalcitrant and Beckett was running out of money. He translated some poems for Edward Titus, who needed them for a Surrealist number of his magazine *This Quarter* which André Breton was guest-editing. The September 1932 issue, featuring the work of René Crevel, Benjamin Péret, and such later luminaries as Buñuel, Dali, Tristan Tzara, Man Ray, Tanguy, and de Chirico, was designed to acquaint the English-speaking world with the Paris avant-garde. In his introduction Titus praised Beckett for the excellence of his contributions: "His rendering of the Eluard and Breton poems in particular is characterizable only in superlatives." Beckett had worked for Titus before. In 1930 he had produced translations from the Italian of Montale, Franchi, and Commisso, which appeared in the pages of the magazine the same year they were completed.

The Rosebud Bar, downstairs from the offices of *This Quarter* on the rue Delambre, was Titus's informal meeting place; married to Helena Rubinstein, he enjoyed entertaining his writers there. But now Beckett had a particular reason for seeking out a commission. Following the assassination of the President of the Republic, Paul Doumer, on May 7, 1932, the government was requiring all foreigners in Paris to have a valid *carte de séjour*. Beckett's identity papers were clearly not in order and he could no longer legally stay at his hotel, nor could he register elsewhere. He slept several nights on the floor of Jean Lurçat's studio, Villa Seurat. Remembering that Titus had earlier expressed interest in a translation of *Le Bateau ivre*, Beckett offered to complete some independent work he had done on Rimbaud's poem while still a student at Trinity. Titus paid Beckett £700, not the £1,000 he was hoping for, but it was more than he needed to get him to England. It is hard to say who got the better of the deal. As things turned out, Titus was never to publish Beckett's version of Rimbaud. His magazine ceased publication with the December 1932 number (which included, incidentally, Beckett's short story, "Dante and the Lobster"). *Drunken Boat*, as the Rimbaud translation was called, was not to be published until 1976, under the expert guidance of James Knowlson, a founder of the Beckett Archive at the University of Reading in England. Beckett's plans, too, went similarly awry. He arrived in London and found a place to live near the Gray's Inn Road, but nothing came of his plans to write for Fleet Street or the more serious literary reviews. When Titus's money ran out, he was forced to return to Ireland.

Back in Dublin, Beckett lived on the top floor of his father's office building on Clare Street, opposite Greene's Bookshop. He began shaping some of the material from *Dream of Fair to Middling Women* into *More Pricks Than Kicks*, the collection of short stories published by Chatto and Windus in 1934. Though the title cites no less a source than the Acts of the Apostles, 26:14 ("Saul, Saul, why persecutest thou me? It is hard for thee to kick against the pricks"), the work would be banned at home, number 465, in fact, on the Irish censorship lists. The book consists of nine episodes in the life of a young Dubliner called Belacqua, while the tenth installment, "Draff," is devoted to the third Mrs. Shuah, who becomes his widow. The hero, as the *Times Literary Supplement* pointed out on July 26, 1934, is "a queer creature, a very ineffectual dilettante, much given to introspection and constantly involved in clownish misfortunes." The review was quick to notice the "implicit effect of satire," obtained in this case "by embellishing the commonplace with a wealth of observation and sometimes erudition, alternated with sudden brusqueness. Belacqua is more a theme than a character, an opportunity for the exercise of a picturesque prose style." Though the stories were "uneven," the project, according to *TLS*, was not without merit:

31   *André Breton as photographed by Man Ray, c. 1928–29*

32   *Paul Eluard, Karel Teige, and Jacqueline and André Breton in Paris, 1933*

"there is a definite, fresh talent at work in it, though it is a talent not yet quite sure of itself." The opening story in *More Pricks Than Kicks* is "Dante and the Lobster." It ends with Belacqua, who that morning had been "stuck in the first of the canti in the moon," arriving after his Italian lesson at his aunt's house. The hero is hungry, but nonetheless concerned with the crustacean's last moments:

> "You make a fuss" she said angrily "and upset me and then lash into it for your dinner."
> She lifted the lobster clear of the table. It had about thirty seconds to live.
> Well, thought Belacqua, it's a quick death, God help us all.
> It is not.

In 1986 Beckett told Barry McGovern, who did a dramatic reading of the story for Irish radio, that he would now reconsider this abrupt conclusion. After listening to a tape of McGovern's recitation, he let the young Irish actor know that "maybe" he would "change" the last line. It might read, he suggested, more Dantesque as follows:

> Well, thought Belacqua, it's a quick death, God help us all.
> Like hell it is.

While he was working on his short stories in his garret lodgings on Clare Street, Beckett also edited the verse published by Europa Press (1935) in a volume originally called *Echoes Bones and Other Precipitates*. The title comes from Ovid's *Metamorphosis* (iii, 341–401) and the cycle of poems, based in part on Provençal forms, mostly conveys a recoil from "this clonic earth." Beckett's writing was becoming, especially to conservative Irish eyes, as "bohemian" as himself. His parents had long ago given up the idea that he would enter the family business with his brother Frank, who did what was expected of him when he returned from India. Beckett had already thrown to the winds what had once promised to be a brilliant academic career. According to Deirdre Bair's unauthorized biography, May Beckett never reconciled herself to the failure of bringing her younger son to heel. Then, on June 26, 1933, almost without warning, his 61-year-old father collapsed and died after a massive heart attack. "What am I to do now," Beckett despaired, "but follow his trace over the fields and hedges."

William Beckett left his son a small annuity of £200, which was enough to get him back to London. Beckett took a furnished room off the King's Road at 48 Paulton's Square, Chelsea, where he stayed for almost three years. This was a hard time for him, "bad in every way, financially, psychologically." Peggy

33, 34   Above: *The front room on the top floor, and* below, *the garret, of 6 Clare Street, where* Beckett *wrote* More Pricks Than Kicks *and began the novel* Murphy *in the early 1930s. The offices of Beckett and Medcalf, quantity surveyors, were located downstairs.*

35　Beckett's cousin Peggy Sinclair, who died of tuberculosis on May 11, 1933, at the age of 22. She was the daughter of Beckett's Aunt Cissie, his father's youngest sister, and William ("The Boss") Sinclair, the son of a Jewish family in Dublin. Between 1928 and 1932 Beckett travelled six times to visit the Sinclairs in Kassel, Germany, where his uncle was an art dealer.

36 W.R. Bion,
Beckett's psychoanalyst
at the Tavistock Clinic
in London

Sinclair, the cousin to whom he had long been attached, had died of tuberculosis only a month before his father's death. Soon her father, William Sinclair, a favorite uncle, was also dead from the same disease. Beckett was with him during his last days at the Wicklow sanitorium. In London he began to consult W. R. Bion (1897–1979), a young doctor who was to become known for his work on the use of group process and group therapy for the rehabilitation of RAF flyers. At the time Beckett saw him at the Tavistock Clinic during 1934–35, Bion had not yet qualified as a psychoanalyst, though he was to serve years later as President of the British Psychoanalytic Society (1962–65) before settling in Los Angeles. During the two years Beckett was Bion's patient, he found his novel *Murphy* impossible to complete; writing, among other things, was not going well. According to Mary Manning Howe, "He did, you know, really have a breakdown." The novel we read today reflects, in part, Beckett's experiences during this uneasy period. *Murphy* urges us to consider, for example, the environs of the Magdalen Mental Mercyseat located "on the outskirts of London," an institution for "the better-class mentally deranged." When its hero meets his accidental and ignominious end, however, his ashes are supposed to be deposited back home in Ireland—and in the men's toilet of the Abbey Theatre. But the plan miscarries. Murphy's remains find their final resting place amid the sawdust of a Dublin pub.

The chapters shift scenes back and forth between Ireland and England, tracing Beckett's own movements at the time. He came back to Foxrock, only to leave once more. Ireland was the land, he wrote, of his "unsuccessful abortion." But London was not the solution. "They always know you're an Irishman," he said. "They call you Pat." During one of his extended stays in Dublin he had "a really sad love affair" with Betty Stockton, the lovely 20-year-old girl from a wealthy family whom his friend Mary Manning Howe had brought with her from America. "He fell madly in love with her," but "she just brushed him aside . . . But he never forgot her . . . it made a dent." On his next retreat from Ireland he travelled in Germany, and finally returned to Paris in the fall of 1937. A year later he had moved into the small apartment at number 6, rue des Favorites, which was to be his home until 1961. He was done with Ireland, except for the occasional visit. His was not to be, then, a Joycean exile. He observed much later, "I just slipped away."

37 *Beckett with his brother Frank, and Suzanne, at Ussy-sur-Marne in 1952*

38 Right: *The rue des Favorites in 1941. In 1938 Beckett moved into a small apartment at number 6, his Paris home until 1961, when he moved to larger quarters on the boulevard St. Jacques.*

In January 1938 Beckett was attacked on the streets of Paris. Late one night a pimp named Prudent accosted him on the avenue d'Orléans and demanded money. Beckett refused, and found a knife plunged into his chest. He later confronted his imprisoned attacker and asked him why he had been selected as a victim. "Je ne sais pas," his assailant replied. In *Waiting for Godot* the playwright assigns this line to the Boy, who signals the closure of each act with his enigmatic response to Vladimir's search for certainty: "I don't know, sir." While he was recuperating from his serious wound, a pianist at the Paris Conservatoire named Suzanne Dumesnil, six years older than Beckett, came to visit him in the hospital. Later she would become his wife, though they were not officially married until 1962. Their relationship, though childless, has endured for more than 50 years. The couple have divided their time between Paris and their modest country house in Ussy-sur-Marne, about 30 miles from the capital.

By the late Thirties Europe was preparing for war and Beckett had still not made his mark as the writer he hoped to become. He described these years as a period of profound "lethargy and apathy." *Murphy* was finished, but it had been rejected by Jonathan Cape, the Hogarth Press, Grayson, Gallimard, and even by the publisher of *More Pricks Than Kicks*, "Shatton and Windup" (Chatto and Windus), before Routledge, through the intercession of Herbert Read, brought it

39 "La Coupole," one of Beckett's favorite meeting places in the Quartier Montparnasse.

out in January 1938. Dylan Thomas, reviewing the novel for the *New English Weekly* on March 17, observed that its author was "a great leg-puller and an enemy of obviousness." But he also noted that Beckett had created a fiction which "never quite knows whether it is being told objectively from the inside of its characters or subjectively from the outside." Like many subsequent readers, Thomas was puzzled by the fact that Beckett had developed a story in which the reactions are the characters' while the manner in which they are presented belongs to a ubiquitous narrator. Complicating such technical problems as point of view and the limits of individual consciousness, Beckett makes us see Murphy and his world through an intermediary consciousness, the unidentified but omniscient narrator who is intimately acquainted with the motivations and reasonings of each personality. Beckett, too, seems to have been aware of his problems with narrative perspective. "All the puppets in this book whinge sooner or later, except Murphy, who is not a puppet," he writes with uncharacteristic candor halfway through the story. Even the novel's first sentence exhibits its author's trouble with the contingencies of a clumsy form: "The sun shone, having no alternative, on the nothing new." Beckett's weariness, however, is not so much with the world at this point as it is with the word. After Joyce, especially after the Joyce Beckett knew in *Work in Progress/Finnegans Wake*, how might it still be possible to write a novel? "Joyce had a profound effect upon me," Beckett once admitted. "He made me realize artistic integrity."

Beckett's encounter with Joyce, however, can only be held partially responsible for his delay in finding his own voice, in a language of his own. Not an acolyte by temperament, Beckett also had to free himself from the echoes and influences he had accumulated during his long years of academic preparation at Trinity. In *More Pricks Than Kicks* and *Murphy*, as well as in most of the poems written during this period, he had not yet found his way through such "loutishness of learning." "A very fair scholar I was too," his narrator casually admits before advertising his knowledge of Milton's cosmology in *From an Abandoned Work*, "no thought, but a great memory." Beckett's writing of the Thirties displays an alarming *préciosité* at odds with "the itch to make." He had come to modernism late; unlike Joyce, but like T. S. Eliot, he had also come to it with the handicap of professorial fussiness. His hero in *More Pricks Than Kicks* borrows his name as well as his disposition from Dante: Belacqua, whose "bliss" comes by sitting and waiting. Even the Irishman Murphy, partial to rocking chairs, suffers the same sedentary fate. Behind Beckett's writing of these years lurks the suspicion that perhaps there is really nothing more to be done, at least not by *this* aspiring author. Things had already been made new. Beckett, moreover, was still writing in English, though he had attempted French in a few of the poems composed in

40 *Beckett seated in a Paris* café, *December 1985*

Paris. And he was still writing prose and poetry, not plays. On a visit to Ireland he filled three notebooks, now in the critic Ruby Cohn's possession, with plans for a dramatization of Dr. Johnson's relationship with Mrs. Thrale. All that came of this project, however, was a fragment in one scene called *Human Wishes*. By the time Joyce was Beckett's age, he had already published *Portrait of the Artist as a Young Man* and was hard at work on his next major project, *Ulysses*.

Beckett was still at home visiting his mother when war was declared in Europe. He returned to Paris. "I preferred France in war," he told Israel Shenker of *The New York Times*, "to Ireland in peace." As a citizen of neutral Ireland, Beckett might have remained in Paris with impunity, even after German tanks invaded the city. But since, as he said, the Nazis were making "life hell" for his friends, he agreed to Alfred Péron's invitation to serve as microphotographer and translator for the Resistance, a commitment to action which later won him the Croix de Guerre. "I couldn't stand with my arms folded," he admitted years later. Beckett worked on captured documents detailing the movement of Axis troops for an underground cell called *Gloria*; the materials were then smuggled into Free France and flown to Allied headquarters in London. Of the more than 80 members of Beckett's unit, only 30 were to survive the war. Under torture a member of the group broke down and revealed the names of his comrades. A telegram from Mme. Péron was delivered to Beckett's apartment, warning him to go into hiding, but it remained unopened; Alfred had been arrested. (Beckett's friend died at the end of the war in Switzerland, soon after his liberation from Mauthausen concentration camp.) Suzanne also had trouble with the Gestapo. When she found the SS at the apartment where she had gone to warn friends, she told the storm troopers she had come for her cat. The SS followed her home, where she fended them off by waving the copy of *Mein Kampf* she kept on a bookshelf. Beckett spent several anxious weeks in occupied Paris before he found a *passeur* willing to engineer his escape to the south, where Suzanne had relatives in Avignon. He spent the remaining years of the war in Roussillon, a small village near Apt in the Vaucluse, waiting.

While hiding out from the Nazis, Beckett continued what he called his "Boy Scout work" for the Underground. In Roussillon he was something like a post office box for the Resistance, getting messages from one person to another. Diversons were few. In this picturesque town, famous for its red clay, Beckett could play chess at the Hôtel Escoffier with the painter Henri Hayden, another refugee from Paris, or drink wine with the local farmers, Aude and Bonnelly. The latter is mentioned by Vladimir in *En attendant Godot* (but not, as it turns out, in *Waiting for Godot*): "Nous avons fait les vendanges, tiens, un nomme Bonnelly, à Roussillon." After he and Suzanne spent several months in the local hotel, she

found a small house for them at the edge of the village. They moved there in 1943 and it was there that Beckett wrote *Watt*, one more attempt at a novel in English.

In *Watt*, not published until 1953, we meet the titular hero at the house of the mysterious Mr. Knott. Beckett's reader encounters two "high-class nuts to crack": chronology and point of view. The novel is presented in four parts, but each of its "heroic quatrains" undermines the narrative authority established in the other sections. There are agonizing "limits," as Beckett states in the Addenda, "to part's equality with whole." We read, too, that "Obscure keys may open simple locks but simple keys obscure locks never." Originally called *Poor Johnny Watt*, the story features the first of Beckett's figures to move with a "funambulistic stagger" and the first of them whose need is for "semantic succour." In the kitchen Watt spies a pot, but was this indeed a pot of which one might say, so to speak, "Pot, pot, and be comforted"? Learning little, or perhaps nothing, Watt departs as he arrives, in summer. In Part I he is compared to a "roll of tarpaulin" and in Part IV he is dismissed as "the long wet dream with the hat and bags." In Part III language itself begins to break down, first word order, then words themselves. Is this Ireland or is this a madhouse? We learn only that Watt and "Sam" live in "pavilions" or "mansions," Boswell's word for the cells of Bedlam previously mentioned in *Murphy*. Watt eventually makes his way into a bedroom, but what strikes him there is an abstract painting which serves as an emblem for the work as a whole. Was this a circle in search of a center or a center in search of a circle, "in boundless space, in endless time"? Permutations and combinations notwithstanding, Watt finally concludes that yes, this is a circle in search of a center, and yes, this is a center in search of a circle: only this center is not looking for this circle and this circle is not looking for this center. So much for Descartes. It is "a tiring style," as Beckett earlier wrote of Proust, "but it does not tire the mind." And one final caution, the last line of the book: "no symbols where none intended."

Although Beckett once dismissed *Watt* as "a game" and "a joke," he also said, in a more reflective mood, that it was a way of "staying sane" and a means "to get away from war and occupation." He was among the first to join the Irish Red Cross after Allied forces landed in Normandy. This was merely a ploy, he said modestly at the time, to get him back to his Paris apartment. In the town of St. Lô he served as interpreter and storekeeper from August 1945 to January 1946. Six months later, on June 10, 1946, he read a script on Radio Erin, defending the mission of the Irish Red Cross Hospital, where he had worked, against allegations of waste and mismanagement levelled at it back home. The title was borrowed from a book of photographs which showed St. Lô before the night it was bombed and afterwards, June 5 and 7, 1944. His broadcast was called, simply, "The Capital of Ruins." Beckett had returned to liberated Paris. His apartment, his books, and his desk had been left mercifully intact.

42 *Beckett, standing at left, with members of the Irish Red Cross Hospital Staff in St. Lô, Normandy, September 1945*

43, 44 Below left: *St. Lô Square before the blitz, and* right, *the ruins of St. Lô after the bombing, June 1944*

45   *Samuel Beckett in 1957*

2

By now there is something almost legendary about Beckett's postwar years in Paris. Between 1946 and 1950 he wrote, in addition to *Waiting for Godot*, the trilogy of novels, *Molloy*, *Malone Dies*, and *The Unnamable*; the three short stories, "The End," "The Calmative," and "The Expelled," as well as the much longer "First Love"; the prose tale *Mercier and Camier*; the *Texts for Nothing*; and an unpublished play called *Eleuthéria*, whose title is the Greek word for freedom. He had abandoned English and was working in a foreign language, as he said at the time, "pour faire remarquer moi." "Perhaps only the French language can give you the thing you want," remarks Belacqua's friend Lucien in the "virgin chronicle" *Dream of Fair to Middling Women*, "perhaps only the French can do it." To the critic Herbert Blau, Beckett confided that French "had the right weakening effect"; to another, Richard Coe, he said that he was afraid of English "because you couldn't help writing poetry in it"; and to still another, Nicklaus Gessner, he admitted that in French it was easier to write "sans style." He told Israel Shenker that he switched to French because he just felt like it. It was a different experience from writing in English. "It was more exciting for me—writing in French." The change in language, however, also marked an important change in artistic direction. Beckett had finally found a way around "saying the same old thing in the same old way." In his fiction he was becoming a practitioner of what was soon to be called the "new novel."

Beckett's work in French during his most prolific period reflects an imaginative world that moves progressively inward. Although this retreat from external action is noticeable in the English writing he did up to the end of the war, the journey charted there is often in the hands of a narrative authority who remains safely outside of the story itself. "I think Murphy spoke now and then, the others too perhaps, I don't remember," Beckett writes self-reflexively in *The Unnamable*, "but it was clumsily done, you could see the ventriloquist." In French Beckett recedes much further into the self; now the narrator, as Hugh Kenner observed, is "narrated." The remarkable stylistic maturity is, however, more a question of vision than technique, Beckett's own evaluation of Proust's imaginative breakthrough. In *Mercier and Camier* Beckett still holds on to the kind of objective storyteller who *seemed* so convincing in dictating the movements of *Murphy* and *Watt*. But in this tale, of which the author once said "the less said the better," Mercier and his Dublin friend Camier are no longer going places. In the French manuscript they travel only "autour du Pot dans les Bosquets du Bondy." In colloquial French the grove of Bondy is a den of thieves and *tourner autour du pot* is "to detour." The movement this French speaker details with such formal aplomb is in reality a journey to nowhere and back again.

Camier, "small and fat, red face, scant hair, four chins, protruding paunch, bandy legs, beady pig eyes," is Oliver Hardy; Mercier, "a big bony hunk . . . hardly able to stand, wicked expression," is Stan Laurel. Together these vaudevillians recall the "hardy laurel" we have previously met in *Watt*. Francis Xavier Camier, a Soul-of-Discretion detective like the Jacques Moran we encounter in *Molloy*, has a rendezvous with a Mr. Conaire, listed as an "hors d'oeuvre" in the French text. Mercier is his intrepid Watson, prénom indeterminable, a delicate and hypersensitive soul unhappily married to the nonappearing Toffana, a very tough Anna Livia Plurabelle indeed. No matter how far the pair roam, they are never far from a woman named Helen, on whose Kidderminster carpet playful murmurings can be heard during long, damp forenoons. We are in Ireland and, more particularly, in the area immediately surrounding Dublin with its canals. Saints Patrick and Teresa work in a barroom owned by Mr. Gast and managed by Mr. Gall, the latter making a return engagement from his role as piano-tuner in *Watt*. Sleuth and chum are invited to down a couple of pints with Watt, the hero who will drink only milk during his sojourn at Mr. Knott's house. Although Watt says he knew one of the two in the "moses basket," neither Mercier nor Camier remembers him. "I knew a poor man named Murphy," says the Proustian Mercier, "who had a look of you, only less battered of course. But he died ten years ago, in rather mysterious circumstances. They never found his body, can you imagine." "I am not widely known, true," says Watt, "but I shall be, one day."

Mercier and Camier is a series of sudden encounters framed by the laws of chance, that terrorist tactic preached as a Dada-surrealist aesthetic. The pair meet by chance, a tossed umbrella determines the road they will take, and it is only by chance that they miss seeing one another at the story's impossible conclusion. "Chance knows how to handle it," says Mercier, "Deep down I never counted but on her." The sudden shifts effected by chance move us along from one music-hall routine to the next. Orchestrating the laws of chance, while never obeying its strictures, is Beckett's narrator, the "I" we discover on the first page. He passes

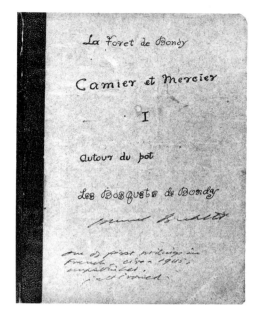

46 *Autograph manuscript, signed 1946, of* Mercier et Camier. *Beckett's note reads: "One of the first writings in French, circa 1945, unpublished, jettisoned."*

47 *"Angel Voice Music" from the original typescript of* Watt

48 *A page from the autograph manuscript of* Malone Meurt, *with revisions, deletions, and characteristic doodles. Dated at the beginning "27 November 1947" and upon completion "30 May 1948," the novel was originally entitled* L'Absent.

49 One of the 945 pages in the autograph manuscript of Watt, written in ink and colored crayons. The first of six notebooks contains the following note: "Watt was written in France during the war 1940–45 and published in 1953 by Olympia Press."

with alarming fluidity in and out of the chapters, twelve in the French edition Beckett withheld until 1970, eight in the English translation which appeared four years later. ("I'll weaken some day," Beckett told a sympathetic critic who had urged him to publish the story long before then.) Despite the summaries at the end of every two chapters, resembling the Addenda to *Watt*, we never learn why things mysteriously disappear: parrot, umbrella, raincoat, pen, sack, bicycle, finally friendship itself. The narrator has given us information only ornamentally, and there are, of course, things he has chosen not to reveal. He will tell us, for example, virtually nothing about himself, only that he was with Mercier and Camier "all the time." The narrator who emerges in Beckett's short stories of the same period will have a great deal more to say for himself. His dialogue from now on will be in league primarily with itself. Recoiling from the confusion of the outside world, Dublin or elsewhere, Beckett focuses our attention on the far greater mystery within. Work in regress has suddenly yielded a new possibility for Beckett's work in progress.

"To contrive a little kingdom, in the midst of the universal muck, then shit on it, ah that was me all over." Stream-of-consciousness never sounded like this before. In fact, it is not really stream-of-consciousness at all, but rather the evocation of a *voice*, specifically a writer's voice, crying out for communion in a purely fictional wilderness. And it is, of course, in *Molloy, Malone Dies*, and *The Unnamable* that this voice will reach for its greatest impact. Beckett came upon the idea of a trilogy only in midstream. He had originally thought of two books, not three. But the notion of ending on a novelistic knockout, with his writer-hero in *Malone Dies* apparently dead, proved unsatisfactory. It gave death a dominion too self-consciously theatrical and the work itself a pattern almost conventional, far too sentimental for what Beckett had in mind. "It's vague, life and death," says Malone as *he* lies dying. "I have lived in a kind of coma," this "moribund" had observed even earlier. "The loss of consciousness for me was never any great loss." A voice from beyond the grave might provide the right tone here, especially if it were to come from some unnamable realm where "finality" is literally "without end." With the prospect of three novels in mind, Beckett was forced to add a crucial clause to that long second paragraph which brings expansion as well as closure to the first part of *Molloy*. "This time, then once more I think," the revised first sentence now reads, "then perhaps a last time, then I think it'll be over, with that world too."

Beckett's trilogy is a major conception as well as a major achievement in the history of the novel. In working on this project he turned his back once again on the remnants of the realistic mode, preferring instead to explore the boundaries of a totally hermetic sphere. He had long ago derided the inadequacy of Balzacian illusion, "solution clapped on problem like snuffer on a candle." Joyce's excavations in form had in any case drawn the curtain on that particular option. *Molloy* begins with its title hero talking, alone in a room he has only recently acquired. He is, in fact, neither *here* nor *there*. "I am in my mother's room. It's I who live *there* now." "I don't know," he continues, "how I got *there*" (emphasis mine). What follows is the gigantic roundabout answer to a question nobody asked. In Part I Molloy, who "always had a mania for symmetry," sets out in search of his mother and ends up in a ditch: "Molloy could stay, where he happened to be." In Part II we meet the Frenchified Irishman Jacques Moran, whose task is to track down and shadow the elusive Molloy. His report begins circumstantially: "It is midnight. The rain is beating on the windows." Moran, however, gets lost, in the forest as well as in prose. His fate is to return home, a failure, reduced to a pathetic Molloy-like state. "It was not midnight," Beckett concludes. "It was not raining." This is circularity with a difference, the cycle undermining rather than completing itself. For in *Molloy* nothing happens, or rather nothing happens in the way it used to in the novels written up to then. This is a circle, alas, whose circumference never meets. "The will has been opened," the unnamable utters, "nothing for anybody."

What urges the reader along in *Molloy* is the curious disconnection of similitudes. This ties the two sections of the novel together and adds metaphysical resonance to what might otherwise be a purely intellectual puzzle. Certainty, like Godot, is nowhere to be found. It has been replaced, instead, by the search for certainty, a journey that guarantees the "incurious seeker" no return. The danger, as Beckett said of Joyce, is in "the neatness of identifications." The reader must be constantly on guard against "committing reason." There is a wicket-gate in Part I and a wicket-gate in Part II. Both Molloy and Moran have names that begin suspiciously with the letter M. Molloy carries a rusted clasp-knife; Moran puts a similar object into his own pocket. Moran's investigation begins just after a gong strikes in his house, the same sound Molloy hears as he lies helpless in a ravine. Moran travels to a town called Bally, while Molloy is moving to a place he knows merely as B or P. Molloy tells us that the man who collects his writing every Sunday is always thirsty. Gaber visits Moran on a Sunday and drinks a German beer called Wallenstein; on his return the very next Sunday, he "announced he was dying of thirst." Molloy speaks of a son he may have forgotten; Moran, accent on the first syllable, is finally deserted by the son he has mistreated. Both men attach their hats to their collars with a shoe lace; both rest their stiff legs to dislodge clots; and both are troubled by their testicles, which in each case "hung a little too low." Both say they know nothing about botany. Moran takes morphine and Molloy thinks Lousse is drugging his food. Both cannot "on any account

50　*Barry McGovern performing a celebrated passage from* Malone Dies *in his one-man Beckett revue called* I'll Go On, *originally presented at the Gate Theatre in Dublin.* ". . . in winter, under my greatcoat, I wrapped myself in swathes of newspaper. . . . the Times Literary Supplement was admirably adapted to this purpose. Even farts made no impression on it."

resist a bicycle." And both are finally unsettled by the question, "What are you doing?"

Malone Dies takes the problem one step further. While Molloy and Moran cast a retrospective glance at the travels that have got them nowhere, Malone's "unreal" journey is the adventure of writing itself. His plan is to end his life and his story at the same time: "I wonder what my last words will be, written, the others do not endure, but vanish, into thin air." Malone is familiar not only with Molloy and Moran, but with the whole "troop of lunatics" that includes Murphy, Mercier, and several figures from *Watt*. To these he adds his own creation, Macmann, the subject of one more tale to while away the time until his "old debtor," death, transforms fiction into ultimate reality. "My life, my life," Molloy had complained, "now I speak of it as of something over, now as of a joke which still goes on, and it is neither, for at the same time it is over and it goes on, and is there any tense for that?" Within the confines of *Malone Dies*, moreover, death is shown up as the sham it inevitably is: merely one more technical device in the employ of any fictionalizer. Malone can't die any more than Macmann can. Each remains part of an emerging fable in the process of storytelling that is likely to go on forever. "Moll, I'm going to kill her," says Malone. She dies three pages later, but only when her author, in this case Malone, in the hands of *his* author, Beckett, chooses to write her out of the story. Moll's funeral, then, like Malone's, is strictly a grammarian's. "True lives," we read on, "do not merit this excess of circumstance."

Malone therefore makes quite a "mess" of his decease. And the bungle becomes even more glaring with his abrupt reincarnation as the voice who speaks in *The Unnamable*. Here Beckett restricts even further the paraphernalia of fiction, on the celebrated "principle of parsimony" that less can sometimes be more. "The artistic tendency," he had written in *Proust*, "is not expansive, but a contraction." Concentration on a single voice leads to a "wordy-gurdy" without the intrusion of plot, personality, landscape, etc. The word becomes the hero. What results sounds abstract, but is anything but that in the new novel Beckett has created. "All those Murphys, Molloys and Malones do not fool me," this disembodied voice self-righteously intones. "They have made me waste my time, suffer for nothing, speak of them when, in order to stop speaking, I should have spoken of me and of me alone." This loquacious nonperson is on a search too, this time for an authentic pronoun. The "vice-existers" he had used before needed artificial props, like the Venus pencil and the exercise-book which became Malone's life. Worse still, Molloy had needed that much-maligned red-herring, a mother, to set him on his way. No wonder they never got anywhere. In *The Unnamable* Beckett has written himself out of these masks of fiction. Paring down this last of his three novels to what a story has always been, a voice speaking aloud, his final sentence becomes the closest thing to heroism we're likely to get in contemporary writing:

> . . . you must go on, I can't go on, you must go on, I'll go on, you must say the words, as long as there are any, until they find me, until they say me, strange pain, strange sin, you must go on, perhaps it's done already, perhaps they have said me already, perhaps they have carried me to the threshold of my story, before the door that opens on my story, that would surprise me, if it opens, it will be I, it will be the silence, where I am, I don't know, I'll never know, in the silence you don't know, you must go on, I can't go on, I'll go on.

The Unnamable, nevertheless, brought Beckett to another impasse. The work, he said, "finished me or expressed my finishedness." He began to talk at the time of having no "nominative," no "accusative," and no "verb"; no "I," no "have," and no "being." In French he called "The End," "The Calmative," and "The Expelled" *nouvelles*, not the word to describe a novel, and he borrowed the title of *Textes pour rien* (*Texts for Nothing*) from "mesure pour rien," a musical term signifying a bar's rest. These works were nothing more than "the grisly afterbirth of *L'Innommable*." "Short abortive texts," they "express the failure to implement the last words" of *The Unnamable*. He was, he observed, "not so much bogged down as fogged out." "I felt the need to create for a smaller space," he explained in 1983, "one in which I had some control of where people stood or moved, above all of a certain light." He turned to a play in the interval between *Malone Dies* and *The Unnamable*, he told Colin Duckworth, "as a relaxation, to get away from the awful prose I was writing at the time." Asked why he decided to work on a play in the midst of writing fiction, Beckett replied: "I didn't choose to write a play. It just happened like that." He was "in search of respite from the wasteland of prose." But in 1985 he provided further clarification: "I wrote *Godot* to come into the light. I needed a habitable space, and I found it on the stage."

51 *Beckett directing Beckett in 1984, with Walter Asmus at lower right. The playwright is shown here at the Riverside Studios in London, recreating in English the Berlin* Warten auf Godot *he staged in 1975.*

52   *Beckett variation by Tom Phillips, 1984*

3

In 1949 Beckett attended a performance of *The Ghost Sonata* mounted by the then unknown Roger Blin. He did not go off to the Gaîté Montparnasse casually. Suzanne had previously given Blin the *Godot* typescript, and Beckett had heard that the director might be interested in doing his show. He went back a second time to look at this low-budget interpretation of Strindberg's paean to dreams and obsessions. Though the houses were small, the production, Beckett said, was true to the play, both to the "letter" and to the "spirit." This pocket theater might provide, then, the proper venue for Gogo and Didi's stage debut. Not that Beckett had had all that much choice. Suzanne had offered the manuscript to several other theater managers, but they had all systematically turned her down.

It took Blin nearly three years to find a house in which to stage *Godot*. The Gaîté Montparnasse, where three of Blin's shows had already been box office disasters, was in deep financial trouble. It closed its doors in 1951, leaving Blin holding most of the bills. For a while it seemed that the play might move into the Poche on the corner of the rue de Rennes and the boulevard du Montparnasse, with an opening announced for late summer 1952. But the 60-seat theater had an unexpected hit in Sacha Pitoeff's production of *Uncle Vanya*. When the run of Chekhov's play was extended, the manager unceremoniously cancelled the contract with Blin. In the meantime *Godot* had appeared in print. The publisher Jérôme Lindon, who had purchased from Vercors (pseudonym for Jean Bruller) the old equipment of his clandestine underground press, brought out a preproduction version of the play in 1952. He also offered Beckett the imprint of Les Editions de Minuit for his novels. After Suzanne had been given the run around by each of the editors she hoped to interest in the trilogy as well as *Godot*, she was relieved to find someone who saw "quelque chose génial" (something of genius) in *Molloy*. Since then Lindon has remained the publisher for all of Beckett's work in French. He has, in advance, already been named Beckett's literary executor.

53 Left: *Frédéric O'Brady as Hummel and Roger Blin as the Student in Blin's production of Strindberg's* La Sonate des Spectres (Ghost Sonata) *at the Gaîté Montparnasse in 1949*

55 Right: *Beckett and Jérôme Lindon, his publisher at Les Editions de Minuit*

54 *The Théâtre de la Gaîté-Montparnasse under the Occupation*

Short of cash, Blin reluctantly applied to a government agency for a grant. He learned that subsidies might be made available to a director willing to produce the work of a foreign author writing for the first time in French. With the enthusiastic support of poet-playwright Georges Neveux, who served on the selection committee, Blin received 500,000 old francs. He still did not have a theater—nor did he have very much money. The old francs translated into not much more than $1500 or £800. The actress Delphine Seyrig, who long admired Blin and who would later star in such Beckett works as the French versions of *Play*, *Come and Go*, and *Footfalls*, came into some money and promptly became one of *Godot*'s angels. By the end of 1952 Blin had persuaded Jean-Marie Serreau to schedule Beckett's *Godot* at his newly opened Théâtre de Babylone on the boulevard Raspail. The house was four times as large as the Poche, but the stage was, fortunately, just as small. *En attendant Godot* had its world premiere there on January 5, 1953. It ran for more than 100 performances.

At the Théâtre de Babylone, Roger Blin found himself playing his own Pozzo after the actor he had rehearsed for the role left the show two weeks before it opened. Having lived with the play for so long, Blin, a skillful trouper, was naturally familiar with all of the parts. He had earlier done a dramatic reading of snatches of Vladimir's and Estragon's dialogue on a radio program broadcast in Paris in February 1952. Yet when he finally had a chance to do *Godot* on the stage, he thought it "improper to question the author about its meaning." He was

61

absorbed, instead, by the more practical matters of "traps, false trails, and allusions," as well as by the characters' "physical defects." "I know there are different levels in *Godot*," he declared, "but the desired magic can be attained only by first dealing fully with the most immediate human level." Blin was also concerned with blocking his players around a rock, a solitary tree, and a country road. The playwright was not much help to him here. "The only thing I'm sure of," Beckett told his director, "is that they're wearing bowler hats." Blin once stated that the play originally caught his eye because it seemed relatively inexpensive to stage. On first reading, he admitted, its wider significance completely eluded him, though he did say that he found the cabaret patter rather attractive. *Eleuthéria*, which he was also considering at the time, was, by contrast, a monster to produce. The dramatic narrative in this case is divided into three acts spread over three consecutive days. It calls for a busy simultaneous set and a large cast: seventeen characters, among whom we meet an Oriental torturer, a glazier, a man of science and another of letters, as well as a Stoppardian Spectator who comments on the plot as it laboriously unfolds. Even with actors assigned to more than one role, *Eleuthéria* would be an impossible work to showcase in the little theaters struggling along on their shoestring budgets on the Left Bank. In this unlikely extravaganza we meet Victor Krap, a soporific hero who spends most of the play in bed, with his back to the audience. His bourgeois parents move in a social circle featuring supporting roles unfortunately labelled Piouk and Meck (*mec* is French slang for pimp). There is also a love interest, the mercurial Olga Skunk. *Eleuthéria*, much commented upon though not as yet published, has never been performed.

In Paris the first *Godot* was something more than a succès d'estime. The play was reviewed, if not understood, by nearly all of the critics who mattered, and the

56, 57   Lucien Raimbourg as Vladimir, Pierre Latour as Estragon, Roger Blin as Pozzo, and Jean Martin as Lucky, in the 1953 world premiere of En attendant Godot *at the Théâtre de Babylone in Paris*

reviews were mostly favorable. Jean Anouilh's evaluation, which linked the importance of the opening night at the Théâtre de Babylone to the Paris premiere of Pirandello's *Six Characters in Search of an Author* staged by Pitoeff in 1923, is perhaps the most memorable. In the pages of *Arts-Spectacles* the playwright called the new work a "music-hall sketch of Pascal's *Pensées* as played by the Fratellini clowns." From the outset Beckett's play was to have an international appeal. Elmar Tophoven, a student from Germany, translated the script into his native language. By the fall of 1953 his translation was running at the Berlin Theater Festival, only a few months after Blin's French production had toured Germany. *Godot* crossed the English Channel on August 3, 1955, when, backed by Donald Albery, Peter Hall's production opened at the Arts Theatre Club (it transferred later to the Criterion). The first London audiences reacted more coolly to the play than had their counterparts on the Continent until the two leading newspaper critics turned things around. "It is bewildering," Harold Hobson wrote in his famous review for *The Sunday Times*. "It is exasperating. It is insidiously exciting." Urging his readers to go and see Beckett's new play, Hobson told them that they would discover there "something that will securely lodge in a corner of your mind for as long as you live." In *The Observer* Kenneth Tynan was uncharacteristically euphoric, labelling himself a *godotista*.

58 Left: *The English language premiere of* Waiting for Godot, *directed by Peter Hall at the Arts Theatre Club in London (1955), with Peter Bull as Pozzo, Timothy Bateson as Lucky, Paul Daneman as Vladimir, and Peter Woodthorpe as Estragon*

59 *Beckett's American director, Alan Schneider*

In 1956 Alan Schneider brought *Waiting for Godot* to America. The circumstances were at first propitious. He had seen the play in Paris and even though, in his own words, his French was "just good enough to get me in and out of the American Express," he knew quite clearly that you "didn't have to understand French in order to react." *Godot*, he said, "had me in the beginnings of a grip from which I have never escaped." He was Beckett's most dedicated director in the United States and died tragically in May 1984, struck by a motorcycle in London while crossing the busy road just outside the Hampstead Theatre. He had just posted a letter to Beckett in Paris.

Michael Myerberg, the original producer for *The Skin of Our Teeth* in 1943, wanted to bring *Waiting for Godot* to Broadway—starring Bert Lahr and Tom Ewell. His first choice for director was Garson Kanin, but when "Gar" was unavailable, he turned to Schneider, whose New York revival in 1955 of the Thornton Wilder play he much admired. Although Schneider had some reservations about the project—and he said so a year or so before to another potential producer, Robert Whitehead—this time, as he admitted in his autobiography, "somehow I couldn't say no." Myerberg insisted that Schneider meet with the playwright in Paris; on the same trip he could also look in on Peter Hall's production, which was still running in the West End. Beckett said he could spare "the New York director" only half an hour. Schneider asked the first question: "Who or what is Godot?" Beckett stared off into space, then responded in his upper-class Dublin accent: "If I knew, I would have said so in the play." Schneider closed his notepad; things improved. So much so that Beckett volunteered to accompany Schneider to England.

65

The playwright was not cheered by what he saw in London—and he saw Peter Hall's production five times. The stage was too busy, the narrative too slow, the statements too meaningful, and the comedy too broad. The director confessed to Michael Billington in 1988 that his *Godot* was "probably far too cluttered and full of extraneous effects." "It's ahl wrahng!" Beckett said about a particular bit of stage business or the recitation of a certain line. "He's doing it ahl wrahng!" In 1974, when Hall was directing Peggy Ashcroft in *Happy Days* at the National Theatre, Beckett told him that "all true grace is economical." But Beckett did not find much "grace" or much economy in the first English-language production of *Godot*. Nor would he have found much in Schneider's American version, which soon turned into a major fiasco.

60 *Beckett, Jean-Marie Serreau, and Albert Giacometti during rehearsals for the 1961 revival of* En attendant Godot *at the Odéon in Paris*

61   Lucien Raimbourg, Etienne Bierry, Jean-Jacques Bourgeois, and Jean Martin in the 1961 Paris Godot, *directed by Roger Blin on a set designed by Giacometti*

Myerberg had the idea of opening the play in Miami and billing it as "the laugh sensation of two continents." He hoped to capitalize on the presence of his big star, Bert Lahr, as well as on Tom Ewell's recent commercial success in *The Tunnel of Love* and *The Seven Year Itch*. But when the play opened at the Coconut Grove on January 3, 1956, the first night audience, led by Walter Winchell, walked out in droves. Tennessee Williams and William Saroyan, however, stayed on; when the curtain finally came down on act two, they greeted the work as well as the cast with a generous "Bravo!" *Godot* eventually made it to Broadway a few months later, but this time with a new Vladimir—as well as a new director. E. G. Marshall replaced Tom Ewell and Herbert Berghof, who had already done a workshop production of the play at his New York studio, restaged the show for its premiere at the John Golden Theatre, where it opened on April 19. The play ran for ten weeks. Each night there were organized discussions between actors and audience, the first time this had ever occurred at a Broadway theater. Kurt Kasznar and Alvin Epstein were memorable as Pozzo and Lucky, but the production itself, despite some positive reviews, never fully recovered from the Florida debacle. "Playing *Waiting for Godot* in Miami," Bert Lahr reminisced, "was like doing *Giselle* at Roseland."

Godot survived the Coconut Grove, and it was to survive, too, the many interpretations, adaptations, transformations, modifications, and even mutilations to which it has become subject as it entered the repertory of world drama.

62, 63   Alec McCowen as Vladimir and John Alderton as Estragon, with (right) *Terence Rigby as Pozzo in Michael Rudman's 1987 production of* Waiting for Godot *at the National Theatre in London*

Giving the lie to Walter Kerr's summary dismissal of the work as "intellectual fruitbowl," *Godot* has been made into an opera, a television movie, and the occasion for two dance recitals: one called *May B*, performed by the French troupe Maguy Marin, and another called *La Espera*, choreographed by Rolando Beattie and performed in 1987 at the Teatro de Bellas Artes in Mexico City. There is even an unauthorized sequel called *Godot Came*, written in 1966 by the Yugoslav playwright Miodrag Bulatovic. Pozzo and Lucky were cast as a Jew and an Arab in an Israeli production in Tel Aviv, and Brecht wanted to change them into landowner and peasant in the Marxist counterplay he thought of writing before he died. The play has, of course, been the center of an unending stream of critical and philosophical inquiry, and Martin Esslin used it as his first example of the new postwar drama he called "the theater of the absurd." Writers as different as Harold Pinter, Alain Robbe-Grillet, Athol Fugard, Sam Shepard, David Mamet, Eugene Ionesco, Tom Stoppard, Vaclav Havel, Caryl Churchill, Friedrich Dürrenmatt, and Maria Irene Fornes have expressed in various ways their indebtedness to *Godot*, and even the indomitable Lillian Hellman, when asked in 1972 about which plays she liked to follow, answered simply, "Everything by Beckett." Arthur Miller, too, has recently, if somewhat grudgingly, admitted that in *Godot* "that playwright was up to something universal." And it was largely on the basis of the play's reputation that Beckett was awarded the Nobel Prize for Literature in 1969, becoming only the third Irish-born writer, after Shaw and Yeats, to be so honored. Characteristically, Beckett deferred to Joyce: "The prize should have gone to him."

64 *Louis le Brocquy, who illustrated the limited edition of* Stirrings Still, *designed the 1988 production of* Godot *at the Gate Theatre in Dublin, with Barry McGovern as Estragon and Tom Hickey as Vladimir.*

65 Right: *The director Mike Nichols at the piano during rehearsals for the 1988 Lincoln Center production of* Waiting for Godot *at the Mitzi Newhouse Theater in New York, with Steve Martin (Didi), Robin Williams (Gogo), Bill Irwin (Lucky), and F. Murray Abraham (Pozzo)*

In *Waiting for Godot* Beckett succeeded in writing a lyrical play for an age that had almost nothing poetic to say for itself. The scene in which "nothing happens, twice" was somehow not merely diagnostic, but prophetic: it was suddenly mankind, not just any poor player, who was waiting for something to arrive which never comes. The lines echoed recent European history, but they also had at their core the substance of myth. Beckett was with the empyrean. *Godot*, in Alan Schneider's words, was something more than a play. It had become, he wrote, "a condition of life." And yet it is in the practical realm of theater that the play continues to live, the real test for any drama that claims, like this one, to be a modern classic.

The play has therefore proved to be more resilient than anything that has been done to it. On November 25, 1987, Michael Rudman's new production, starring Alec McCowen as Vladimir, John Alderton as Estragon, Terence Rigby as Pozzo, and Peter Wight as Lucky, opened at the National Theatre, London. A year later Mike Nichols' much-anticipated *Godot* opened for a seven-week run in New York. Plans were in the works to make a film version of the Nichols' *Godot* for television. *A country road. A tree. Evening.* There were still some new audiences for *Godot* to conquer.

66   *Beckett in Giacometti's studio with the tree the artist designed for the 1961 Paris revival of* Godot

4

As a piece for performance *Waiting for Godot* can be daunting in its lonely simplicity. It marks the direction Beckett's writing for the theater would take over the next 40 years. Stage space, simultaneously discreet and striking, would be exploited tactfully and richly. The single tree, for example, is arresting, evoking both life and knowledge. When Estragon thinks of hanging himself there, the same prop becomes an emblem for death, betrayal, perhaps even crucifixion. At the beginning of act two, when we discover a few hopeful leaves, there is also, quite unexpectedly, redemption and rebirth. All the dead voices, we hear in this play, make a noise "like leaves." Trees, at least Beckett's, can also be funny. Estragon tries to imitate one: "Gogo light—bough not break—Gogo dead. Didi heavy—bough break—Didi alone. Whereas—." On this platform Beckett's solitary "willow" has therefore been of considerable use to his players. "Everything's dead," Vladimir concludes, "but the tree." A simple lighting cue emotionalizes the setting and adds metaphysical resonance: when the sun sets and the moon quickly rises, artificial yet real, we know all at once that this cycle is destined to repeat itself. Pozzo was right. Time, Beckett's stage time, has not stood still. The ritual of performing this play, or of watching its drama unfold, suddenly implicates us in one more act of renewal.

The set is therefore empty but filled with suggestion as Beckett tries "to make the frozen picture of waiting into the major motif of the play." Beckett's actors make his set speak a complete vocabulary of stage business. Theirs is a repertory of spontaneity: commedia dell'arte, music-hall skits, crazy pratfalls, pantomime, cabaret banter, actors "acting," onstage meals, dances, sight gags, rope tricks, songs. Characters think and characters fart. They also smoke, beg, reminisce, fall asleep, drink, and kick. They salivate, urinate, procrastinate. They take off their shoes. They try on their hats. They carry suitcases and picnic baskets. They dream. They go away—and they come back. They remember the Bible, not exactly chapter and verse perhaps, but certainly the more colorful illustrations. "One of the thieves was saved" after all, this script's welcome and very

67, 68 *Beckett at the Royal Court Theatre during rehearsals for Anthony Page's 1964 revival of* Waiting for Godot. *This was the "first unexpurgated version" of the play performed on the London stage.*

"reasonable percentage." And, like Winnie in a later play, at least part of their classics remains, especially those bits that sound so much like Virgil and Heraclitus. Their lines are nourished, too, by faint recollections of Dante, Shakespeare, Calderón, Shelley, Dickens, Schopenhauer, Verlaine, Berkeley, Hölderlin, Joyce, and Yeats (the list is not complete). It was just such an allusive texture that made the critic Vivian Mercier tell Beckett, "You make Didi and Gogo sound as though they have Ph.Ds." "How do you know they hadn't?" was the playwright's prompt response.

In public, however, Beckett has consistently downplayed any attempt to define a work that was "striving all the time to avoid definition." "My work is a matter of fundamental sounds (no joke intended) made as fully as possible," he wrote to Alan Schneider in 1957, "and I accept responsibility for nothing else. If people want to have headaches among the overtones, let them. And provide their own aspirin." Insisting always "on the extreme simplicity of dramatic situation and issue," Beckett would much rather talk about where a character sits or stands than what "exegesis" might make of him. In *Waiting for Godot*, as Hugh Kenner pointed out, such weighty hermeneutics "disturb no surface texture." The play can be accessible without them, though they do offer the "local situation" a great deal of comic irony—not to mention the sad ring of recognition, if not truth. *Godot* features what the playwright once called the "perpetual separation and coming together of Estragon and Vladimir." Although his 1975 director's notebook for the Berlin Schiller-Theater production speaks of this pattern as cruciform, Beckett has nonetheless denied any specifically religious reading of the play: "Christianity is a mythology with which I am perfectly familiar, so naturally I use it." "If by Godot I had meant God I would have said God, and not Godot," Beckett told Ralph Richardson, who once considered playing the part of Vladimir in London. "This seemed to disappoint him greatly."

And yet the play offers us something more than the stark romanticization of a question mark. An alternating tempo of laughter and tears is clearly and consistently developed as we move on from one "little canter" to the next. Every act of comic deflation, however, will be undermined by stage silence, which can speak as eloquently on this set as any line of dialogue a character has been assigned. Beckett explores just how little has to happen onstage for a lyrical mood to "expand" and quite overwhelm the rising dramatic tension:

Was I sleeping, while the others suffered? Am I sleeping now? To-morrow, when I wake, or think I do, what shall I say of to-day? That with Estragon, my friend, at this place, until the fall of night, I waited for Godot? That Pozzo passed, with his carrier, and that he spoke to us? Probably. But in all that what truth will there be? *(Estragon, having struggled with his boots in vain, is dozing off again. Vladimir looks at him.)* He'll know nothing. He'll tell me about the blows he received and I'll give him a carrot. *(Pause.)* Astride of a grave and a difficult birth. Down in the hole, lingeringly, the grave-digger puts on the forceps. We have time to grow old. The air is full of our cries. *(He listens.)* But habit is a great deadener. *(He looks again at Estragon.)* At me too someone is looking, of me too someone is saying, He is sleeping, he knows nothing, let him sleep on. *(Pause.)* I can't go on! *(Pause.)* What have I said?

(He goes feverishly to and fro, halts finally at extreme left, broods. Enter Boy right. He halts.)

Silence.

Vladimir's soliloquy, for his summary of the play's major events is precisely that, isolates man on the cosmic plane which is also "the Board" of this stage. Here frail humanity is as brutally "unaccommodated" as it had earlier been in *King Lear*, a much larger play of epic proportions. Though they have added another level of complexity to the greater complexity Didi addresses, all those connections to a world outside this drama have really got us nowhere. They present us with no key, they offer us no solace, and they provide us with no easy way out. In the theater they do help us, of course, to pass the time, which the characters assure us would have passed anyway. We are left with bits and pieces, centers that cannot hold, fragments that yield no comforting form. There is, miraculously, still no reason to despair. For in this play Beckett shows us that the emptiness of experience can also be its fullness. Godot doesn't come, but a young boy returns in his place. The struggle resumes. The question of voices has been superseded by a more somber vision: the question of going on. In the meantime, pants fall down. Vladimir's climactic speech is, then, the true prayer at last, "the prayer that asks for nothing." Things are looking up; Gogo pulls *on* his trousers. "Everything's dead but the tree."

"All is" finally "corpsed" in Beckett's next stage play, *Endgame*, which Beckett dedicated to Roger Blin. A darker work than *Godot*, and much darker in English than in the original *Fin de partie*, the play borrows its title from the same game of chess that inspired Eliot in *The Waste Land*. Here Beckett tightens the cord. For an endgame is a serious reduction of forces, as Marcel Duchamp wrote in *Opposition and Sister Squares Are Reconciled* (1932), his famous study of a chess match. The fewer the players, however, the greater the tension. Blin's French production, featuring himself in the role of Hamm, had its world premiere in

69   *Alfred Lynch and Nicol Williamson as Gogo and Didi in the 1964 London revival*

London on April 3, 1957 (the company played later that same month at the Studio des Champs Elysées in Paris). George Devine had planned to direct the first English version of the work at the Royal Court Theatre, but when Beckett's translation was still not ready by March, as promised, he persuaded Blin to bring the play to Sloane Square. Performing in French for the English Stage Company was, as the playwright said, "rather grim, like playing to mahogany, or rather teak." In October 1958 Devine portrayed Hamm in his own production at the Royal Court, but by then Alan Schneider had already done *Endgame* in New York. It opened at the Cherry Lane Theatre in Greenwich Village on January 28, 1958. Still, Beckett told Nancy Cunard, Blin's French production "was more like what I wanted, nastier."

Beckett said that *Endgame* was "difficult and elliptic, mostly depending on the power of the text to claw." The play was, he thought, "as dark as ink." He conceived an early version of the piece in two parts. The first act closed on the

70, 71   Roger Blin as Hamm and Jean Martin as Clov in Fin de partie (Endgame), *performed in Paris at the Studio des Champs Elysées in April 1957*

LORD CHAMBERLAIN'S OFFICE,
ST JAMES'S PALACE, S.W.1.

8th January 1958.

Dear Mr Devine,

"End-Game"

I write in reply to your letter of January 7th, in which you say that Mr Beckett feels that he cannot make an alteration to the passage on page 28.

In the circumstances the Lord Chamberlain will not be able to grant a Licence for the public performance of this Play.

Yours sincerely,

G.Devine Esq.

72   Signed letter from the Lord Chamberlain's Office dated January 8, 1958, to George Devine of the Royal Court Theatre, refusing a license for a public performance of Endgame *unless certain changes were made in "obscene" and "blasphemous" passages in the script. "I think this does call for a firm stand," Beckett wrote from Paris. The license was finally granted on August 6, 1958, but only after lengthy negotiations between Beckett, Devine, and Lord Scarborough's staff.*

73 *Nell and Nagg in the Royal Court* Endgame, *1958*

apparent death of Nell, with the second act opening on the line Hamm lifts from Prospero's speech in *The Tempest*, "Our revels now are ended." But the division proved unsatisfactory. Bringing the curtain down on poor Nell was certainly theatrical, but it was just as certainly melodramatic. It drew far too much attention to her final withdrawal from the onstage action. The two-act structure also violated the mood of claustrophobia central to this work in performance. There is, for audience as well as player, simply no exit. The cyclical pattern Beckett uses to so much effect in *Waiting for Godot* depends on the spectator's apprehension of a rhythm of return. Repetition, especially repetition with a difference, sustains dramatic tension and enhances that play's rising action. Variation on a theme builds not only contrast, but conflict. But in *Endgame*, which the playwright called "more inhuman than *Godot*," all cycles have just about run their course. "Finished, it's finished, nearly finished, it must be nearly finished," the play's opening line, is delivered "*tonelessly*." This will be a theatrical spectacle of reckonings "closed" and stories "ended."

74　*Patrick Magee and Jack MacGowran as Hamm and Clov in the 1964 London revival of* Endgame *by the Royal Shakespeare Company at the Aldwych Theatre*

That opening line is ripe with the promise of closure. Here Beckett quotes, or rather deliberately misquotes, from John 19:30. "It is finished," Jesus' ultimate exit line, has been in this case refashioned for the "bare interior" of a tableau that is anything but vivant. Hamm, a diminutive Hamlet played by a ham actor, keeps his "accursed progenitors," Nell and Nagg, in trashbins. Clov (to rhyme with *glove*) serves a master of ceremonies who may very well be *his* own father. But the play of generations, like everything else in this work, is winding down too: Beckett names his petty tyrant after the wayward Ham Noah condemns in Genesis to an eternity of servitude as well as despair. "Cursed be Canaan," father tells son in that prophetic "chronicle." The names Beckett's protagonists wear carry other suggestions no less ominous. In this endgame blind Hamm is the hammer that drives all the nails: English *nail* is French *clou* and German *Nagel*. Beckett has, of course, used such bilingual puns before. His cast for *Godot* is literally "all humanity": Slavic Vladimir, formerly Jewish Lévy; French Estragon, like clove, also a spice; English Lucky, perhaps so-called, the author said, because he has "no expectations"; Italian Pozzo, a fountain of learning (as in *è un pozzo di sapienza*) but also a *pozzo nero*, a cesspool. Didi and Gogo have also been seen, less efficaciously perhaps, as ego and id. The nonappearing Godot has been similarly tagged. While his name resembles Charlot, French for Charlie Chaplin, it is also a bilingual pun on God and water (French *eau*).

75   *The 1984 production of* Endgame *at the Samuel Beckett Theatre in New York, with Alice Drummond as Nell, James Greene as Nagg, Alvin Epstein as Hamm, and Peter Evans as Clov*

How much of Beckett's international name-game can be accommodated in performance has always been subject to question. In *Endgame*, for example, it does very little to lighten the tone of the play. From the beginning the work has presented an enormous challenge to any director: how to evoke an essentially tragic posture without sacrificing Beckett's bitter, irreverent, often outrageous humor. "Nothing is funnier than unhappiness, I grant you that," Nell says parenthetically, yet her statement has been far more difficult to organize in practical stage space. Most interpretations of *Endgame*, in the theater as well as in criticism, have given up on comedy and gone for the tragedy instead. The result has been a production history far more checkered for *Endgame* than anything awaiting *Godot*. In 1978 Rick Cluchey enlisted Beckett's help for the San Quentin Drama Workshop production. Despite the playwright's assistance, the show was short on humor and long on existentialism. On tour in London a few years later, the show dragged on for nearly three hours   not the "hour and a quarter" one-act the playwright had in mind when he wrote to Schneider in the 1950s (in a subsequent letter he amended his timing to "over an hour and a half"). Beckett directed the play himself in Berlin, where for rehearsal purposes he divided *Endspiel* into sixteen scenes. "You should never run slowly," he told his German Clov in 1967, "that's very dangerous for the play." In 1973 André Gregory's Manhattan Project presented *Endgame* in New York on a set surrounded by wire mesh. The audience, seated above, looked down on a scene shaped quite differently from the rectilinear enclosure Beckett had in mind. More recently, JoAnne Akalaitis tried to open up the hothouse atmosphere by setting the action in an abandoned New York subway car. Her production, which opened in December 1984 at the American Repertory Theatre in Cambridge, Massachusetts, was threatened by legal action because of the supposed liberties she had taken with Beckett's "explicit" stage directions.

Perhaps the director who has come closest to realizing Beckett's comic density in *Endgame* is Joseph Chaikin. He played Hamm in 1969 in Roberta Sklar's version for the Open Theater, New York, this time taking advantage of the company's skill in voice training and nonverbal performance values. Yet even in this impressive production, sensitive to the musicality of sound and gesture, the accent fell, as Chaikin himself noted, on "the *cry* in it." He returned to the play in 1977, this time as director. When his *Endgame* opened at Princeton University and later transferred to the Manhattan Theatre Club for the 1979–80 season, he decided to examine the work's potential for humor. "One of the primary realities," he said, is "the vaudeville team, keeping the audience *amused* in this play about inertia and despair and deadendedness." Chaikin made his actors and audience discover the intricate way the play patterns "a joke" as "pure joke" before the next "beat" takes them "into a heavy profound thing, then into another joke." For the characters in *Endgame*, Chaikin observed, "There's no wonder; they know everything; there's no more this, no more that. And then something new comes up, and you *explore* it." This play about the end of everything "moves to its own conclusion." Chaikin's breakthrough was hailed as "authoritative" by Mel Gussow of *The New York Times*; Erika Munk in *The Village Voice* called this "the most lucid *Endgame* imaginable." When the show travelled to Paris, the critic for *Le Monde*, Mathilde La Bardonnie, wrote that Chaikin had "penetrated deep enough to find the laugh, the brutal burst of laughter" at the core of the playwright's vision. Beckett, who does not go to the theater anymore, did not see Chaikin's famous *Endgame*, but he did agree to meet the director when he came to Paris. He had heard very good things about Daniel Seltzer's robust and congenial Hamm and he had even sent the actor/professor a note. But by the time that arrived in New York, Seltzer was dead.

Endgame is a constant preparation for leave-taking, "the story of two men who want to leave but who never arrive." Yet in the play Clov *doesn't* leave and Hamm, according to the playwright, "says No to nothingness." Parting is always incomplete: at close of play Clov, the only character who can move, "*remains motionless*," frozen in a brief stage tableau that lasts forever. This is, as Beckett said, "pure play." "It's a cantata," he told Georges Pelorson, "for two voices." As

84

opposed to the openness of *Godot*, this dramatic world is closed in and closing down. When you're trapped onstage you stay, not because you don't want to leave, but because there's simply nowhere else to go: "Outside of here it's death." What you can do, however, is move around the chessboard one more time, and Beckett's players show themselves to be quite adept at that. Clov has the "nice dimensions, nice proportions" of his kitchen, "ten feet by ten feet by ten feet"; Hamm has "the prolonged creative effort" of his chronicle, a work-in-progress in perpetuity; and Nagg has his joke about the tailor and a pair of pants ("I tell this story worse and worse"). "Every man his speciality." Nell, the lone female in this very masculine ensemble, has been given something, too: memories. Beckett's figures therefore stay the course, for in this work "something" is indeed "taking its course." And yet their process of ending, like every other process, is eternal. They may have a little less, perhaps, each time around, but their half is always half of something else: "Old stancher, you remain." This is the dark underside of *Waiting for Godot*. It is also Beckett's preferred play. "I suppose," he said in 1978, "the one I dislike the least is *Endgame*." For in this work the mise-en-scène is more strictly determined to take command of "the greater smallness" that has always been a playwright's interpretive space, the finite boundaries of a stage. *Endgame* cuts much deeper. "In the smaller theater," Beckett said about a Paris revival, "the hooks went in."

In the summer of 1956, when Beckett was still struggling with *Fin de partie*, he wrote to Nancy Cunard about a project he had in mind for a radio play: "Never thought about a radio technique . . . but in the dead of t'other night got a nice gruesome idea full of cartwheels and dragging feet and puffing and panting which may or may not lead to something." He had just been approached by the BBC about the possibility of doing a new script for the Radio Drama Department. Always reluctant to write anything on commission, Beckett told John Morris, Controller of the Third Programme, that he would see if he could come up with something. In Paris Morris was encouraged enough to write Val Gielgud, Head of Drama, that Beckett "has a very sound idea of the problems of writing for radio and I expect something pretty good." *All That Fall* arrived in the mail at Broadcasting House that September.

Beckett's first radio play confronts us with a decidedly Celtic soundscape. This time his work is neither pure French nor pure English, but rather a distillation of all that is "bizarre" in Irish-English. Set in Boghill, the imagined Dublin suburb whose landmarks evoke the playwright's childhood home, *All That Fall* creates a central figure who is, for the first time in Beckett's work, unrelentingly Protestant and unmistakably female: Maddy Rooney née Dunne, "the big pale blur." Overwrought and overweight, she trudges dutifully to the railway station to meet

76   *Ben Halley, Jr. as Hamm and John Bottoms as Clov in JoAnne Akalaitis's controversial staging of* Endgame *at the Loeb Drama Center in Cambridge, Massachusetts. The set for the 1984 production by the American Repertory Theatre included an abandoned New York subway car and*

featured incidental music by Philip Glass. "Any production which ignores my stage directions,"
Beckett wrote from Paris, "is completely unacceptable to me."

her husband Dan. There are no visuals here: she must "sound" fat and he must "sound" blind. Acoustics that have been electronically organized summon up a universe that captures us in our own act of listening. Everything else is dead, "just like our own poor dear Gaelic." But the language we hear in this play is by no means exhausted. Words meet music (Schubert's "Death and the Maiden"); barnyard noises presage dialogue (and vice versa); and mechanically assisted sound announces persons and prefigures properties. Much is heard "onstage," so to speak, but much is heard about an "offstage" world, too. The "Andante" from Schubert's *String Quartet in D minor* is supposed to be heard on a gramophone playing in "that ruinous old house" inhabited by the poor woman Maddy *doesn't* meet on the road. Radio silence, the deliberately perceived absence of sound, punctuates space and marks time. Even the characters' ticket-names are puns which are intended to be heard: the dark Miss Fitt, Mr. Slocum, mad Maddy, and a very lilting Irish surname indeed, Rooney (ruin-y). In this aural landscape "hinnies whinny," moist eyes are "cleg-tormented," and gearboxes get crucified. Maddy quivers like a "blanc-mange," apostrophizes her "corset" as "cursed," and wonders aloud, "Is this cretonne so becoming to me that I merge into the masonry?" Here language has been designated by the author "to come out of the dark." "Beckett is a playwright," the actor Ronald Pickup said in 1986, "who should go straight into your head." Yet the story this playwright tells in *All That Fall* has been composed with its emphasis on recitation, not recounting. To hear is to be perceived. In this medium sound makes all the sense there is.

Beckett's Dubliners are, if nothing else, great talkers. They love the telling as much as the tale. More than that, even, they love to hear the sound of voices, their own as well as others'. "Ramdam!" says Mr. Tyler in a "*marvelling aside*," truly impressed by that special ring of Mrs. Rooney's arcane vocabulary. Here, at last, is someone who knows how to put a bit of "jizz" into it. These roadside reciters are especially eloquent on such grave matters as sterility and the sickness unto death. Mr. Slocum manages to keep his ancient mother out of pain ("That is the great thing, Mrs. Rooney, is it not?"); Mr. Tyler's daughter has had a premature hysterectomy ("Now I am grandchildless"); and Maddy remembers her own lost child, little Minnie: "In her forties now she'd be, I don't know, fifty, girding up her lovely little loins, getting ready for the change. . . ." Voices speak, we listen, noise intrudes its ugly presence: a bicycle tire goes flat, an automobile engine blows a gasket, a hen squawks before meeting sudden death, "her troubles over." The play also presupposes a series of sounds we yearn to hear, but do not, can not, at least not yet: Dan's train from the capital has been unexplainably delayed, a "hitch." On this particular Saturday it's certainly "suicide," as Maddy says, "to be abroad." "But what is it to be at home, Mr. Tyler, what is it to be at home? A

77   The 1987 production of Theatre I *directed by Jonas Salz for the NOHO Theatre Group of Kyoto, Japan, presented a fusion of Kyogen and experimental elements. The actor Akira Shigeyama is at right.*

78 Roger Blin, director, with the actor R. J. Chauffard on the set for the 1960 Paris premiere of
La dernière bande (Krapp's Last Tape)

lingering dissolution." In spite of all this human misery, we hear with bitter irony,
"The Lord upholdeth all that fall and raiseth up all those that be bowed down."
Irish syntax is suddenly upstaged by the sound of a very different language, the
measured cadence of the Renaissance English in the King James version of the
Bible. Dan will join his wife in wild laughter after she announces this Sunday's
text from Psalm 145. For what he longs to do most, or so we hear him say, is "nip
some young doom in the bud." Comedy evaporates, mystery intrudes: a boy falls
from the train carriage and is crushed on the line, under the wheels. "Christ, what
a planet!" This play's life has a cruel way of imitating speech. The Rooneys move
on, mere footfalls amid other sounds: a tempest of wind and rain.

Beckett was in Paris on January 13, 1957, when Donald McWhinnie's BBC
production was broadcast on the Third Programme. He had hoped to hear the
play on his short-wave radio. Disappointed by the fact that there was too much
static on the wire, he wrote to BBC headquarters asking for a tape of *All That Fall*.
The next week he wrote again, this time requesting a manual on how to operate a
tape-recorder. Such is the background for Beckett's next stage venture, a play for
one actor, two voices, and three unities of time.

79 *R. J. Chauffard as Krapp at the Théâtre Récamier in 1960*

Krapp's Last Tape was written in early 1958 for the Irish actor Patrick Magee (an early draft of the piece is in fact labelled "Magee Monologue"). That October Donald McWhinnie's production opened at the Royal Court Theatre on a double-bill with George Devine's *Endgame*. Beckett thought Magee's interpretation of Krapp, which he saw during rehearsals in London, was "terrific." He said this was his "best experience in theater ever." Set in Krapp's den, Beckett's scene for this play begins with a mime accompanied by a wry repertory of amplified sound effects: keys jingle, corks pop, drawers spring, hands rub, feet shuffle, a ledger thumps on a table, a banana peel slithers to the floor. A "wearish old man" heaves a heavy sigh, stumbles, and breathes with difficulty as he moves about this deliberately circumscribed space. But this time we see as well as hear; Beckett's script is now as complicated visually as it had previously been aurally. In this act without words the player's movement has been calculated to hold the stage with authority. Krapp looks at his watch, searches in his pockets, takes out an envelope, puts it back, fumbles again, takes out a small bunch of keys, raises it to his eyes, chooses a key, gets up and moves to front of table. He stoops, unlocks first drawer, peers into it, feels about inside of it, takes out a reel of tape, peers at it, puts it back, locks drawer, unlocks second drawer, peers into it, feels about inside it, takes out a large banana, peers at it, locks drawer, puts keys back in his pocket. He turns, advances to edge of stage, halts, strokes banana, peels it, drops skin at his feet, puts end of banana in his mouth and remains motionless, staring vacuously before him. Finally he bites off the end, turns aside and begins pacing to and fro, meditatively eating the banana. He treads on skin, slips, nearly falls, recovers himself, stoops and peers at skin and finally pushes it, still stooping, with his foot over the edge of the stage into the pit. I am of course repeating Beckett's precise direction for enactment: his mime calls for the complete arrangement of a visual field in perfect harmony with acoustics that are so palpably—and electronically—rendered. In the opening moments of *Krapp's Last Tape* it's as though Beckett has almost succeeded in *visualizing* a radio play's soundscape. "The basic problem of both production and acting lies in the listening," observed Pierre Chabert, who played Krapp under Beckett's direction in Paris. "How can a play which is based on the act of listening be made to work in the theatre? How can the act of listening be dramatized?" "Listening is here communicated," Chabert elaborated, "by the look. It is literally the eye which is listening."

The sight-sound relations at the beginning of the play serve as a kind of prologue for all that is to follow. This is, after all, a performance text that will place its premium on sound. Krapp-at-69 searches for "box three . . . spool five," a tape of thirty years ago. But the occasion for that "old P.M." (post-mortem) was in a sense a reaction to yet another recording session dated a decade or so before, when Krapp was in his twenties: "Just been listening to an old year, passages at random," we hear along with Krapp. "Hard to believe I was ever that young whelp. The voice! Jesus! And the aspirations! . . . And the resolutions! . . . To drink less, in particular." In this play the irony involves three, not two, ages of man. On tape we hear Krapp chuckling at his younger self; onstage we see Krapp laughing bitterly at his recorded laugh. The protagonists in this action, however, are merely two voices: the one we hear recited live by the actor onstage, the other disembodied, but forever imprinted on magnetic tape which the same actor has prerecorded. When Krapp switches on his machine, the audience discovers him in a private act of listening. The sound of his younger voice evokes moments from a past which he experiences anew each time he listens to the tape. Proustian memory is made manifest, tangible, and real. The dynamics is both simple and pointed: we watch Krapp, and we listen with him. The image we see onstage, however, makes an explicit comment on everything that is heard as well as on everything that no longer needs to be said. On this platform every "retrospect" is literally seen in the bitter perspective framed by this mediating tableau. The play

80   *In April 1975 Pierre Chabert played the role of Krapp at the Petit Orsay in Paris*

of voices therefore makes of an intangible past a concrete staged presence. When he picks up a reel of tape, Krapp can even hold his history in his hands. And what remains this time is not some "old stancher," but a "girl in a shabby green coat, on a railway-station platform." The darkness of Krapp's world, and of the audience's bleak horizon, is suddenly illuminated by a verbal image whose visual potential is far more riveting than anything we will see in this stubborn proscenium. A voiced-image on the voice-over defies time. It defines it, too: "The face she had! The eyes! Like . . . *hesitates* . . . chrysolite!" Beckett draws Krapp's simile from *Othello*; fragments from a dramatic past can still be reworked into fresh material for a new repertory. Language can always be counted on to resound in a human voice, the proper vehicle for stage dialogue.

In *Krapp's Last Tape* Beckett's lines still carry the inner determinacy of an Irish melody. Though the playwright once said that "the Krapp text has nothing to do with Dublin," it's Old Miss McGlome Krapp remembers singing ("Connaught, I fancy"); and Krapp's mother, like Beckett's, "lay-a-dying" in a house on a canal that *seems* to be Dublin's. Tired and drunk, this old boozer waxes lyrical. It's his birthday, that "awful occasion," after all: "Be again on Croghan on a Sunday morning, in the haze, with the bitch, stop and listen to the bells . . . Be again, be again." And sex with Fanny, the "bony old ghost of a whore" who "came in a couple of times," is still better than "a kick in the crutch." The Protestant hymn Krapp intones, "Now the day is over,/Night is drawing nigh," foreshadows a twilight that will be once again familiarly Celtic. Several critics have read the Irishness of *Krapp's Last Tape* in a distinctly autobiographical way, especially the "memorable night in March, at the end of the jetty, in the howling wind, never to be forgotten" (Krapp-at-39). On a visit to Ireland to see his mother Beckett is reported to have had some sort of insight on the wharf at Dun Laoghaire resembling his character's "vision, at last" about facing the darkness within. It was like "resolving to go naked," Beckett confided to one friend. To John Calder he said, somewhat apologetically, that it was "something like revelation." Krapp's "crest of the wave," however, is only "— or thereabouts," and Beckett is not Krapp. Whatever Beckett may have experienced on a Dublin wharf during a storm was certainly "less Wordsworthy," to quote from his own *Murphy*. Krapp-at-69 can't stand listening to this overblown passage anyway; the pretension, not to mention the romantic rhetoric of a landscape wallowing in the sublime (complete with lighthouse, foam, and obligatory granite rocks), is simply unbearable. When Krapp is forced to listen to "that stupid bastard" that was himself, he curses before switching off.

Krapp's Last Tape moves not only in time, but through time. Every second in the presentness of performance is quickly turning into Krapp's past. On his

playback Krapp retrieves time; an image memorialized on tape resists mutability. That moment on the lake, in a punt, comes back more than once to "be again, be again," reifying and reasserting his existence in a frail attempt at communion:

I thought it was hopeless and no good going on, and she agreed, without opening her eyes. *(Pause.)* I asked her to look at me and after a few moments— *(pause)*—after a few moments she did, but the eyes just slits, because of the glare. I bent over her to get them in the shadow and they opened. *(Pause. Low.)* Let me in. *(Pause.)* We drifted in among the flags and stuck. The way they went down, sighing, before the stem! *(Pause.)* I lay down across her with my face in her breasts and my hand on her. We lay there without moving. But under us all moved, and moved us, gently, up and down, and from side to side.

Krapp is 69; he has long ago taped his "Farewell to love." This year, like so many others, there is not much news to report, just the "sour cud and the iron stool." The recording we see him make tonight, however, will be his very last tape. The voice from the past might be, finally, prophetic: this earth may soon be "uninhabited." Krapp stares motionless before him as *"the tape runs on in silence."* Who will bother to listen to all those reels when he, too, is gone?

This play, of course, is set in the future. Beckett was worried that his critics might pick up on the fact that, thirty to forty years before 1958 (the date of composition for *Krapp's Last Tape*), there were indeed no tape recorders. He nearly called the work *Ah Well*, the sigh that adds a poetic refrain to so much in his actor's separate but related monologues. In his own production of the piece in Germany, *Das letzte Band*, Beckett decided to place the accent on lyricality by restricting the comic elements specified in his published text. Krapp's purple nose was gone, as was the emphasis on a clown's oversized boots (*"size ten at least"*). But to make sure that the atmosphere might never become maudlin, Beckett kept the slapstick routine of man and cosmic banana, a reassuring touch of humor in this otherwise somber work.

Happy Days brings to a close the first great period of Beckett's writing for the stage. Exploring the "musicalization" of a script in *All That Fall* and *Krapp's Last Tape*, he discovered a new English voice for himself in the live theater. "There is something in my English writing that infuriates me and I can't get rid of it," he said back in 1957. "A kind of lack of brakes." Theater language, oddly enough, seemed to offer Beckett's "strange English" the sort of discipline he needed. *Happy Days* confirms the choice of his native language for the stage and extends its range much further. (Beckett would remain faithful to the English-speaking theater well into the 1980s.) The dramatist Roger Pinget helped Beckett adapt his radio play into French as *Tous ceux qui tombent*, and Pierre Leyris assisted him in bringing *Krapp's Last Tape* to Paris as *La dernière bande*. But he translated *Happy Days* as *Oh les beaux jours* by himself, this time substituting a phrase from Verlaine's "Colloque sentimentale" for the Irish toast he used to name his original version of the play. The English title travelled a similarly literary road; the playwright's early instinct was to call it *Tender Mercies*, a phrase he knew from, among other places, Proverbs 12:10.

Alan Schneider said that Beckett's interest in *All That Fall* and *Krapp's Last Tape* had been in "the sound of a human voice and its power to evoke an entire world." Schneider directed the world premiere of *Happy Days* in New York when the show opened at the Cherry Lane Theatre on September 17, 1961, starring Ruth White as Winnie. Since then the play has provided a remarkable vehicle for an actress, especially one with a strong vocal range. In London Brenda Bruce created the role in George Devine's 1962 Royal Court production, and Madeleine Renaud, who first played Winnie in Paris a year later, made it a staple in her standard repertory (she performed the piece at the Théâtre du Rond-Point as late as 1986). Beckett directed Billie Whitelaw at the Royal Court in 1979, eight years after he staged his own production in German at the Schiller-Theater Werkstatt in West Berlin, with Eva Katharina Schultz as Winnie. Jessica Tandy, Irene

82 *Brenda Bruce, shown here, starred as Winnie in the London premiere of* Happy Days *at the Royal Court Theatre in 1962, directed by George Devine. In 1979 Beckett directed Billie Whitelaw on the same stage in his own production of the play.*

83 *Madeleine Renaud as Winnie in* Oh les beaux jours *at the Odéon in Paris, 1963*

84   Alan Webb as Willie and Peggy Ashcroft as Winnie in the final moments of the National Theatre production of Happy Days. *The show opened at the Liverpool Playhouse on November 26, 1974, and joined the NT's London repertory at the Old Vic in March 1975.*

85   Right: Peter Hall with Peggy Ashcroft on the set for the National Theatre production of Happy Days. *Beckett, invited to attend rehearsals, urged the director to remember that "all true grace is economical."*

Worth, Peggy Ashcroft, Siobhan McKenna, Nancy Illig, Marie Kean, Beatrice Manley, Hanna Marron, and, more recently, Aideen O'Kelly have offered their own very different virtuoso interpretations of this "well preserved" earth mother, the "blond for preference" literally planted in the ground.

Happy Days is pure scenography: in this play you can't separate character from set. Buried up to her waist, then up to her neck, Winnie is part stage design, part stage protagonist. She is both acted and acted upon: the earth claims a lot more of her in act two, and Willie, "dressed to kill," will "mount" her with great difficulty in a tantalizing parody of what a play's denouement is supposed to be. Beckett's image of Winnie, conceived with a "maximum of simplicity and symmetry," resembles the final frame of *Un chien andalou*, where the camera uncovers human figures similarly "stuck" in "the bleeding ground." Beckett knew the Buñuel-Dali filmscript at least as early as 1932, when it appeared in the same number of *This Quarter* as his own contributions. Perspective in *Happy Days* relies on cinematography in other ways, too: our first view of Winnie, from the waist up, is a theatricalized counterpart of a camera's medium-shot, while her descent into the mound in act two, "imbedded up to neck," offers us the stunning contour of a filmic close-up. Scene design in *Happy Days* is therefore the indispensable collaborator in any interpretation of this work. Here Beckett creates a dramatic text which approximates the actual stage picture in mood as well as in physical detail. He first conceived *Happy Days* as a play in one act, but he later divided the action, not quite proportionally, into two separate sections. A one-act structure would mean losing a crucial resonance no theater practitioner would want to miss: a visual contrast which frames the whole conflict of the play.

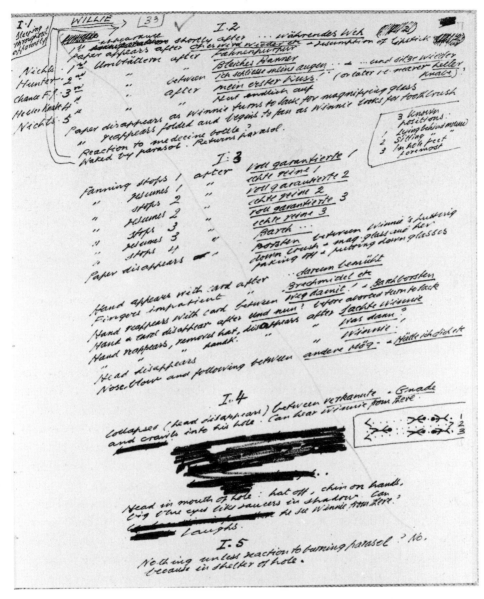

87 *A page from Beckett's 1971 production notebook for* Glückliche Tage (Happy Days), *which he directed at the Schiller-Theater Werkstatt in Berlin*

86 Left: *Human figures buried in the earth in the final frame of* Un chien andalou (1928), *directed by Luis Buñuel from a scenario by Buñuel and Salvador Dali*

In *Happy Days* the light-dark contrast of *Krapp's Last Tape* gives way to "blazing light" on a trompe-l'oeil backcloth "to represent unbroken plain and sky receding to meet in far distance." Here lighting will be used to create a sense of depth on an otherwise shallow proscenium. This is a deliberately stark—and staged—reality. Although *Happy Days* is a two-character play, the work is, in effect, Beckett's first female solo. Willie is less player than prop, an excuse for Winnie to begin her day as well as the catalyst for her monologue: all she wants to know is that she is not speaking into the void. "Just to know you are there within hearing and conceivably on the semi-alert is . . . er . . . paradise enow." Beckett once said that he selected a woman for this role because the contents of a handbag would provide an immobile character with more "business" to do onstage. And yet this statement belies his growing fascination with the vocal range of a female player, the quality of sound he was able to get from an earthy Maddy Rooney, an ethereal Miss Fitt, or a sentimentally "canned" but philosophically correct Nell. In *Krapp's Last Tape* his solo had been designed for a solitary masculine register, alternately metallic and live, but fundamentally bass, baritone, or tenor. *Happy Days* exploits the higher timbre of Krapp's female counterpart, a vocalizer whose rising action climaxes in a song of songs, the waltz duet from *The Merry Widow*.

Beckett called Winnie "a mess," but "an organized mess"; she isn't "stoic," he continued, she's just "unaware." He told the director Shivaun O'Casey, the playwright's daughter, to keep the rhythm down, "not to make Winnie too capable a woman." A "bird with oil on its feathers," "Win" begins her day conventionally, with prayer. A bell signals the call to action, abruptly awakening this player into the harsh light of stage consciousness. The playwright originally intended to use an alarm clock instead of a bell, but such a localized prop would undermine the efficacy of an offstage agency as goad for the unfolding drama. Malevolence lurks in the wings, the same mysterious force that will ultimately bury Winnie even deeper into her stage space. Winnie's spirit is impressive; she creates a cozy domesticity out of limited resources. Things are running out, to speak in "the old style," but she nevertheless summons up a repertory of gestural energy to get her through each "heavenly" day. Her skills in body movement, first arms, hands, neck and head, then eyes, lips, and mouth, prevent the play from becoming static. On this platform a parasol even burns up, accompanied by flames and smoke. Willie makes the most of his cameo appearances, too, restricted as he is to a view from behind the mound. But it is language here that plays the most flexible role. When all else fails, words move, and move us, disputing Winnie's charge that "there are times when even words fail." Winnie has her story about Mildred, her report about the travellers Shower or Cooker ("ends in er anyway—stake my life on that"), the sudden discovery of a "live emmet" (Hebrew for

88   *Peggy Ashcroft as Winnie watching her umbrella on fire in the first act of* Happy Days. *The actress said that playing this role for the National Theatre was "like climbing Everest to perform."*

truth), and the memory of a "Mr Johnson, or Johnston, or perhaps I should say John*stone*." "Very bushy moustache, very tawny," she says reverently, "Almost ginger! . . . Within a toolshed, though whose I cannot conceive. We had no toolshed and he most certainly had no toolshed . . . I see the piles of pots . . . The tangles of bast . . . The shadows deepening among the rafters."

Lines from the past will be similarly fragmented, for Winnie, as Beckett said, "is an interrupted being." What she remembers from Shakespeare, Aristotle, Dante, Browning, Yeats, Herrick, Keats, Milton, Samuel Johnson, Charles Wolfe, Edward FitzGerald, the Psalms and Proverbs, and earlier Beckett, is partial. "What are those wonderful lines . . . woe woe is me . . . to see what I see . . . ah yes . . . wouldn't miss it . . . or would I?" she says, a motif she repeats somewhat later when she mangles a line from Thomas Gray's "Ode on a Distant Prospect of Eton College": "you know . . . what is that wonderful line . . . laughing wild . . . something something laughing wild amid severest woe." Even gravity isn't what it used to be; Winnie has a great fear that if the stage did not hold her "in this way" she "would simply float up into the blue." "No better, no worse, no change," she likes to say. But on this stage things are changing, and not necessarily for the "better." That "habitable space" Beckett found in the theater would soon become subject to an even tighter arrangement of the mise-en-scène. Equating stage space with the space of human consciousness, Beckett's drama, like his fiction, moves inward. *Happy Days* makes us see just how much Beckett has been able to do "not only while the performer's mobility was denied but even with a diminishing presence." The remnants of that material presence will become the focus of a remarkable series of theater works that begins with a little play called *Not I*.

89 *Beckett in Paris, December 1985*

90 *Jean-Marie Serreau's 1966 Paris staging of* Va et vient (Come and Go) *at the Odéon, with Simone Valère, Annie Bertin, and Madeleine Renaud. Beckett worked closely with Serreau on this production and a few months later directed his own version of the play in the same theater.*

5

"Can you stage a mouth? Just a moving mouth, with the rest of the face in darkness?" Beckett's speculation about the feasibility of such a daring stage image reveals a heightened commitment to remaking the playwright's space. "The rest," he said, "is Ibsen." In *Play* (1962–63) he elaborated on the ironic stage blocking of Winnie's courageous stability: scenography now features three characters literally potted in identical urns. A bourgeois love triangle never looked like this before. On this set a single spotlight is the anxious prime mover. Light initiates speech, the only conventional action this piece displays. Buried forever in stage time and restricted stage space, faces and urns merge in physical texture as well as in metaphorical essence. *Come and Go* (1965) is equally unsettling. Three seated women perform the most elementary of stage movements: each exits, then re-enters, turn and turn about. As the trio rehearses its series of modest duets, three to the third power, each confidante simultaneously reveals and conceals an exposition indefinitely delayed: "Does she not realize?"; "Has she not been told?"; "Does she not know?" *Breath* (1966) is precisely that: a curtain rises and falls, interrupted by an instant cry the script resolutely labels a "recorded vagitus."

Since *Happy Days* Beckett's theater has been more and more concerned with the relationship between text and performance. His own experience as director signals a change in the very shape of his drama. From *Happy Days* forward, lines of dialogue are written with a technical precision that undermines what might otherwise be their spontaneous delivery. Movement and tempo are similarly predetermined. Stage directions multiply as Beckett begins to challenge the theater's traditional function as a collaborative and interpretive art. When Shivaun O'Casey told him that in her own production of *Happy Days* she planned to use three mounds, Beckett said, "What are the other two for?" About the Akalaitis production of *Endgame* his statement was even more pointed: "Any production which ignores my stage directions is completely unacceptable to me." In a Beckett play "the set, the movements of the actors, the silences specified in

91   *Dianne Wiest, Donald Davis, and Sloan Shelton in the 1976 Arena Stage production of* Play, *directed by Alan Schneider in Washington, D.C.*

92   *Danielle Van Bercheyke, Christian Bouillette, and Huguette Faget in the 1983 Paris production of* Comédie (Play) *at the Théâtre Artistic Athévains*

93   *George Devine's 1964 London production of* Play *at the Old Vic, with Billie Whitelaw, Robert Stephens, and Rosemary Harris.* Play *was restaged at the Royal Court in 1976 on a triple-bill with* That Time *and* Footfalls.

the text, the lighting and the costumes are as important as the words spoken by the actors," wrote Barney Rosset, Beckett's American publisher. What is at stake here is, of course, control, how to translate Beckett's private image into the public forum that is theater. In his work for the stage Beckett has stood firmly for the playwright's, not the director's, prerogatives. "I hate this modern school of directing," he said recently. "To these directors the text is just a pretext for their own ingenuity." "Not for me," he once remarked, "these Grotowskis and Methods." Formal integrity, based in this case on the intimate knowledge and manipulation of sophisticated theater machinery, is once again for Beckett a question of that loaded word "vision," not merely technique.

In *Not I* Beckett's grounding in stage technology has been justly celebrated. What looks at first glance like a radical simplification of style is in fact the result of a complex and highly disciplined scenic arrangement. The visual impact is sensational: a mouth gaping out at us from a void that unexpectedly encroaches on our horizon. Opposing Mouth is a larger than life figure shrouded in the folds of a djellaba, the Auditor who has, according to the playwright, "this kind of pertinent gesture, which is essential." As enacted, Mouth's words pass by quickly, perhaps too quickly for anything approaching recognition in the eighteen minutes Beckett specified for the whole. "I am not unduly concerned with intelligibility," he told Jessica Tandy, who played Mouth in the world premiere directed by Alan Schneider at Lincoln Center in New York in 1972. "I hope the piece may work on the nerves of the audience, not its intellect." In performance, nonetheless, the rhythm and the repetition work on us viscerally and begin to make sense. Beckett's Auditor interrupts Mouth's furious monologue at four climactic points. Raising his arms in what the text calls "a gesture of helpless compassion," this silent and enigmatic figure lessens the motion with each recurrence. Mouth refuses to acknowledge the first-personness of her own story, insisting on impersonality instead: "what? . . . who? . . . no . . . she!" As spotlights fade on Mouth and Auditor, "the buzzing" trails off into the greater incomprehensibility of stage silence: you can't really tell when language is no longer "there." What insinuates its presence, however, is the bold visual image. "You may find nothing in it," said Jessica Tandy, "but I suspect you will never forget it."

That Time, which Beckett called a "brother to *Not I*," is similarly concerned with the problem of fragmentation and theatrical form. A disembodied head hangs suspended in a stubborn proscenium frame, "10 feet above stage level midstage off centre." This time the face is its own auditor as Beckett makes language once again fill the void. Voices A, B, and C, prerecorded, broadcast memories from three set positions, "both sides and above." Here Beckett gives his words an unprecedented spatial presence. Each voice is the same voice, yet each

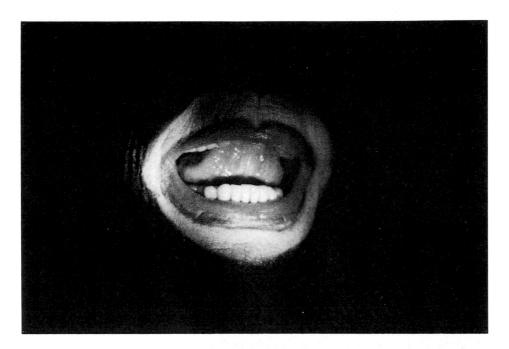

94   Close-up shot of Madeleine
Renaud in Pas moi (Not I) at
the Théâtre d'Orsay, Petite salle,
in 1975. Beckett restaged the play
in the same theater in 1978,
restoring the Auditor, who had
been omitted from his first French
production.

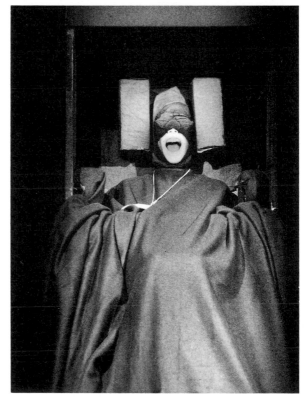

95   Billie Whitelaw on the set
for Not I in Anthony Page's
London production at the Royal
Court Theatre in 1973. The
actress later starred in the
television adaptation of the same
play (BBC, 1976; broadcast
1977).

details a different story chiselled from what the playwright called in *Proust* "the poisonous ingenuity of Time." Stage directions tell us that A, B, and C "modulate back and forth without any break in general flow except where silence indicated." So much technological ingenuity reveals Beckett, ironically, at his most lyrical. Compensating for the language which passes his audience by so rapidly in *Not I*, Beckett now offers us the haunting rhythms of reverie, rest, and remembrance: "that time you went back to look was the ruin still there where you hid as a child. . . ." And yet it is the visual image that once again predominated. Ripe with references to past mythologies, the face of Beckett's Listener confronts us with a new vision of John the Baptist. It is precisely this graphic display which the audience retains long after the curtain comes down. "That time" has disingenuously invaded "our time."

96   Left: *Beckett wrote* Footfalls *for the actress Billie Whitelaw and directed her in the role of May when the play opened in London at the Royal Court Theatre on May 20, 1976.*

97   *Delphine Seyrig in* Pas (Footfalls), *directed by Beckett at the Théâtre d'Orsay, Paris, in 1978*

Patrick Magee played Listener at the Royal Court Theatre in 1976 on a triple bill with *Play* and another new work, *Footfalls*, starring Billie Whitelaw. Donald McWhinnie directed the first two plays, but Beckett staged *Footfalls* himself. This drama features one female figure (May) but two female voices, the one we hear recited onstage, the other we listen to "from dark upstage." In this instance Beckett creates through sound alone his second character, the mother May carries forever with her in her "poor mind." The act of listening is therefore something both personal and sacred; in this play "the motion alone is not enough." Beckett wants us to "hear the feet, however faint they fall," the sound of steps falling through space in time. May paces back and forth, retreading "it all," at once the play's original title, her past psychological history, and her ultimate stage destiny. The mood here is everywhere *diminuendo*, diminishing light, diminishing space, and diminishing sound. Each aspect is a "little fainter," then a "little fainter still," as we move in stage time from one section of the action to the next. Finally, brutally, there is nothing, only an empty space held for the duration of a grim "ten seconds" followed by a fatal "fade out." Yet the picture, as it fades, provides a fixed image, just as the sound, as we remember it, finds its ideal fulfillment. On this platform May's "footfalls," to quote T. S. Eliot, "echo in the memory." In Beckett's *Footfalls* poetry comes, momentarily, to stage life, but we take the image of that poetry with us long after we leave the theater. "My words echo/Thus in your mind." Eliot's line from "Burnt Norton" has been reinvented to fit the intimate scale of Beckett's lyrical proscenium.

Beckett's stage plays of the seventies and eighties demonstrate the profound impact his work for the mechanical media has had on his concept of the mise-en-scène. *Embers*, a play he did for BBC radio in 1959, continues to organize sound within recognizable rules of dramatic action. Unwilled sound keeps thrusting itself forward in the guise of the insistent break of a wave on a shore. Henry's involuntary memory refuses to remain silent. Voices from his dark past materialize as ghostly chords in the uneasy radiophonic present we share with him. *Words and Music* (BBC, 1962) is surprisingly confrontational. In this radio play Croak, a neurasthenic poet, fights hard to orchestrate the two elements of his soundscape, Words and Music, into a solemn artistic experience. Chaos keeps interrupting his attempt to superimpose order on their fitful and sometimes petulant spontaneity. Morton Feldman, who wrote the music for the 1987 production of the play, directed by Everett Frost for the American Beckett Festival of Radio Plays, said that the piece was "close and distant at the same time . . . the closer you get the more tragic it becomes—and the more compelling." In this work the playwright was both "a word man and a note man." *Rough for Radio I* and *II* (early 1960s) further explore the evolution of character through voice and intonation. The first piece remains unproduced, but the second was broadcast on BBC Radio 3 on April 13, 1976, to coincide with the author's 75th birthday. Directed by Martin Esslin, the production featured Patrick Magee, Billie Whitelaw, and Harold Pinter in the role of Fox. *Cascando* (1962), whose title is a musical term meaning "falling tone," is a short piece for melody and voice. The play, originally written, like the *Roughs*, in French, was first broadcast on ORFT-Paris on October 13, 1963, directed by Roger Blin with music by Marcel Mihalovici. A year later Donald McWhinnie's English production was heard on the BBC.

In the visual media Beckett has been similarly analytical and adventurous. In cinema and television he develops highly emotional confrontations from what initially strikes his audience as an abstract and inhuman arrangement of scenic space. Bishop Berkeley's dictum that "to be is to be perceived" is the point of departure for the one script he designed for film. Initially planned as part of a trilogy for Grove Press under the rubric "Project I, Three Original Motion Picture Scripts by Samuel Beckett, Eugene Ionesco, Harold Pinter," *Film* was the only enterprise completed under this grand scheme. Produced in 1964 by Evergreen Theatre, Inc., Beckett's 22-minute "comic and unreal" film starred a wary Buster Keaton under the direction of a not altogether secure Alan Schneider. Beckett made his first and only trip to America to serve as writer-consultant for the project. Set in 1929, the scenario was shot in 35mm black and white on a crumbling site in lower Manhattan not far from the Brooklyn Bridge. On screen Beckett's seedy protagonist is sundered into Object (O) and Eye (E), the former in retreat, the latter in pursuit. The chase-and-escape routines are in

Bill Raymond in the Mabou Mines stage adaptation of Cascando *(New York, 1976)*

this context alternately funny and threatening, but always purely visual: except for the momentary lapse of a "ssh!" this is a silent film in an age that expects state-of-the-art audio-visual effects. The denouement comes when we literally *see* that $E=O$. *Film* is a complete story written in cinematic movement and gesture, the kind of "literature of the un-word" Beckett had in mind when he wrote to his German friend Axel Kaun back in 1937.

99 *Buster Keaton in the 22-minute "comic and unreal"* Film *(1964), directed by Alan Schneider and shot in 35mm black and white. In these frames O stares directly at E in "that look" of surprise and dismay.*

100 *The famous opening shot in* Un chien andalou *(1928) of an eyeball severed by a razor-blade. Beckett's silent* Film *is set "about 1929" and begins with a similarly graphic close-up of an eye: the one hidden by the patch Keaton wears on screen.*

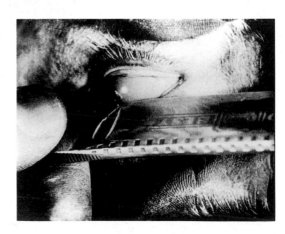

101   Keaton and Beckett on the room set for Film *in New York, July 1964*

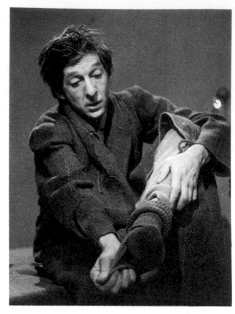

102 He Joe (Eh Joe), *as directed by*
Beckett for Süddeutscher Rundfunk in 1979

103 *Jack MacGowran in the 1966 Eh Joe for*
BBC 2, directed by Beckett and Alan Gibson

Beckett's attraction to video, a more congenial medium than film for presenting the illusion of being inside someone's head, should come as no real surprise. It is, after all, what Beckett himself called a "peephole art." In *Eh Joe*, written in 1965, a fixed position camera follows a silent male figure about a room; discovered alone, he repeats actions we have previously witnessed in *Film*. Once Joe settles down, however, the intrusion of a female voice-over plagues him with the troubling remembrance of things past. "It is a concrete person for Joe," Beckett told Siegfried Melchinger in an interview published in *Theater heute* in 1966 soon after the playwright directed the first of two German versions of the play in Stuttgart. "She really is whispering inside his head. He hears her. Only if she is a living being can he have the wish to kill her. She is dead, but for him she is still living. That is his passion: to kill those voices, which he cannot kill" (my translation). In the 1966 BBC 2 production, starring Jack MacGowran and Sian Phillips, as directed by Beckett and Alan Gibson, the camera dollies-in on a close-up "say four inches each time," accommodating the nine movements called for in the text but all the while emotionalizing the play's essentially geometric shape. The image we see is the same, yet with each camera movement the image is transformed. In this sharp visual field language becomes accusatory, even malicious. Sound cauterizes sight, sight skewers sound.

118

Beckett returned to writing for television in the 1970s with intentions as much musical as mathematical. *Ghost Trio* and *. . . but the clouds . . .* were first broadcast on the BBC on April 17, 1977, on a triple bill called "Shades" which included Billie Whitelaw in the television adaptation of *Not I. Ghost Trio*, which offers the viewer a seemingly endless series of variations on the color gray, also lets us celebrate an environment of rectangles in various sizes. On this screen every rectangle looks the same, but the camera uncovers a fertile aspect to their plane geometry. "Mine is a faint tone," a female voice-over announces wryly. "Kindly tune accordingly." In this "familiar chamber" the three offstage ghosts are voice, camera, and music. For as the male figure anticipates the arrival of a guest, he listens on cassette to the largo from Beethoven's Fifth Piano Trio, op. 70, the one, in fact, popularly known as the *Ghost*. The longed for "she" fails to keep her appointment; a boy comes wordlessly in "her" place. We hear footfalls as his youthful image recedes in darkness down the lonely corridor. Sound is more than incidental: it creates the incident itself. Man must face his ghosts alone.

104   The Boy in Beckett's production of Die Geister Trio (Ghost Trio) *for German television (SDR, 1977). Donald McWhinnie directed Billie Whitelaw and Ronald Pickup in the BBC version, transmitted on April 17, 1977, with* Not I *and . . .* but the clouds . . . *on a three-part program Beckett called "Shades."*

In . . . *but the clouds* . . . Beckett's videotechnology assumes a highly poetic texture. He takes his title from the last lines of "The Tower" by W. B. Yeats, where the "death of friends, or death/Of every brilliant eye/That made a catch in the breath—/Seem but the clouds of the sky/When the horizon fades,/Or a bird's sleepy cry/Among the deepening shades." A masculine voice-over introduces us to one more isolate type, a figure who retreats to his "little sanctum" to don "robe and skull." His rite prepares us for "a begging of the mind," the nightly vigil in which he longs for "her" to appear. This rendezvous with time is purely mental, this tryst imaginary; the black-and-white box renders it diaphanous but nonetheless real. The superimposition of a female face (Billie Whitelaw's in the BBC version) mouths Yeats's lines, finally murmured synchronously by the disembodied voice (Ronald Pickup's, BBC). Two transparencies, image and voice, make Yeats's poetry—and Beckett's drama—concrete. Darkness is redoubled when light fades on these two "deepening shades." Then all is gone, man, woman, voice, picture, "that MINE" of television technology turned lyrical.

105   Alan Schneider's production of Ohio Impromptu *at the Harold Clurman Theatre in New York, 1983. The same show premiered on May 9, 1981, in the Stadium 2 Theater of the Drake Union at the Ohio State University in Columbus.*

106, 107 Right: *Pierre Chabert's 1983 Paris production of* Berceuse (Rockaby), *as performed by Catherine Sellers at the Théâtre du Rond-Point.* Left: Rockaby *at the Samuel Beckett Theatre in New York in 1984, with Billie Whitelaw, who had created the role of W (Woman) in the 1981 world premiere production staged by Alan Schneider in Buffalo, New York.*

In his most recent writing for the theater Beckett has brought his experiences in radio, film, and television to bear on the contingencies of the live stage. *A Piece of Monologue* (1980) reduces his Speaker's voice to the kind of metronomic regularity we normally associate with mechanically assisted sound. *Rockaby* (1981) weaves its lyrical dramatic encounter from the interplay of live and recorded sound. The woman we see onstage, a memory who acts, finally becomes the image we hear described by the Voice offstage. Reader and Listener in *Ohio Impromptu* (also 1981) bring to stage life the very story we hear recited from their "worn volume." In this stark configuration of black, white, and shades of the color gray, each is the counterfeit image of the other. The three plays use light with enormous restraint. Illuminated on a tiny performance space within a wide proscenium, the actor's presence is magnified and enhanced when surrounded by what the theater has traditionally defined as negative space. Each play calls for an economy of gesture where, literally, every breath counts. Blocking is geometric, as tightly controlled as those images Beckett has previously "set" in videotape. Even the rock of a chair is timed to specific units of dialogue. *Catastrophe* (French, 1982), dedicated to the dissident Czech playwright Vaclav Havel, offers us a kind of object lesson in how to make such a dramatic image complete. In this play-within-a-play we watch with ever increasing horror as a Director, collaborating

108 Above left: *Jean-Louis Barrault as the Protagonist in Pierre Chabert's production of* Catastrophe *at the Théâtre du Rond-Point in Paris, 1983*

109 Above: *Alan Schneider's New York production of* Catastrophe *at the Harold Clurman Theatre in 1983*

110 *Antoni Libera's 1986 Warsaw production of his Polish translation of* Catastrophe. *Note the configuration of the Protagonist's left hand, an inverted victory sign for Solidarity.*

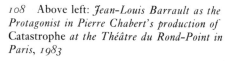

111 Opposite, above: *The world premiere production of* Quadrat 1 + 2 (Quad) *as shown on German television. Beckett said his four players here were "mimes," not "dancers," though the piece was originally composed for the Stuttgart Preparatory Ballet School.*

112, 113 Below: *The dream image in the SDR production of* Nacht und Träume, *which was directed by Beckett in Stuttgart with cameraman Jim Lewis in 1982 and transmitted on German television on May 19, 1983. Off-camera, a male voice sings the last seven bars of op. 43, no. 2, the verse Schubert took from Matthäus von Collin: ". . . come again, holy night!/Sweet dreams, come again!"*

with his Assistant and the offstage "techie" Luke, rehearses his Protagonist in the emblematic role of suffering humanity. "Terrific!" this tyrannical theater practitioner trumpets. "He'll have them on their feet. I can hear it from here."

Technology in Beckett's hands is therefore made to wear a distinctly human face. Although *Quad* (1982), a televisual mime play in color he directed in Stuttgart for Süddeutscher Rundfunk, reduces choreography to a maddening, almost inhuman plane, his next project for SDR, *Nacht und Träume* (1983), uses a mournful melodic refrain to structure tenderness through inference. The only "voice" Beckett needs in this black-and-white video is music, the last seven bars of Schubert's *Lied* (op. 43, no. 2), for which the play is named. The rest is silence, where night and dreams take place. In this play movements on a small screen inscribe meanings that are signifiers without a designate. Like its music, the work offers evocation in place of argument. The same might be said of *What Where*, a play Beckett wrote in French in 1983 but revised in 1986 after he supervised its adaptation for German television in Stuttgart. A work first written for the stage finds a different life in another medium, then comes back to the theater in sharper and revitalized form. Earlier in his career Beckett had insisted on keeping his "genres more or less distinct," but as his writing has progressed it has become difficult, if not impossible, to distinguish mood from mode. The mechanical media provide Beckett's theater with its contemporary vocabulary and lend it an efficient and electronic way of saying more and more with less and less. And though the plays written in this period are typically short, each is essentially timeless. "All of Mr. Beckett's plays are full-length," observed Alan Schneider. "Some are longer than others, that's all, but they're all full-length." These last theater images explore a different aspect of duration, a new way for the performance space to conceive the unity of time. In doing so, Beckett's drama comes full circle. "The light gleams an instant," Pozzo says in *Waiting for Godot*, "then it's night once more."

Opposite

114 Above: *The English-language premiere of Beckett's revised stage version of* What Where, *directed by S. E. Gontarski at the Magic Theatre in San Francisco (1986)*

115 Below: *Beckett's initial stage version of* What Where, *directed by Alan Schneider in 1983, had its world premiere on a triple-bill with* Catastrophe *and* Ohio Impromptu *at the Harold Clurman Theatre in New York. The piece was originally written in French as* Quoi où.

116   *Beckett at the Riverside Studios in London*

6

Beckett's post-trilogy fiction has been similarly concerned with questions of duration, dimension, and scale. "I am not of the big world," Beckett's Murphy had once observed. "I am of the little world." Rigorous and sensual, the work explores epic emotion on a highly restricted verbal plane. "The art of combining is not my fault," we learn in *Enough*. "It's a curse from above." Mostly composed in French, though sometimes written in English, the material in prose develops "a grammar for being elsewhere" which allows us to explore in miniature the tenuous relations separating subject from object. The tripartite structure of *How It Is*—before Pim, with Pim, and after Pim— obscures in English the bald power of a pun in the original French, where *Comment c'est* is also "commencer," to begin. When Pim leaves, the narrator is left waiting for Bom, who will, in turn, reduce him to a Pim-like state, can-opener literally up the anus. Bim-Bom are hardly in this instance the same anti-Stalinist but pro-socialist comedians (the Polish actors Zbigniew Cybulski and Bogumil Kobiela) we remember from a film like Wajda's *Ashes and Diamonds*. The words we have for this fictional journey are, however, "ill-said ill-heard ill-recaptured" and "ill-murmured," all "in the mud." This "script" is shaped as a series of short, run-on units which appear more like stanzas than paragraphs, especially when read aloud. "Something" is always "wrong there," "ill-inspired" or "ill-told." The nameless narrative voice longs to "correct" itself. But before it finally does so, fiction breaks off rather than down. "That's how it is," Pozzo had reminded himself in *Waiting for Godot*, "on this bitch of an earth."

The short pieces which follow *How It Is* have proved far more difficult to categorize. Existing somewhere between poetry and prose, they have perhaps been most adequately described by the Beckett scholar Ruby Cohn as "lyrics of fiction." *Enough* (French *Assez*) introduces us to a speaker of tantalizing bisexuality who documents the breakdown of an impossible relationship made possible in the "art and craft" of telling about it. Recycling Keats, permutations and combinations, and radishes, this work's "ejaculations," "too few for even a

maintained." Qualification is rampant and harmony is elusive. Even the dimensions presented by this seemingly omniscient voice are suspect. David Warrilow, who starred in the Mabou Mines adaptation of *The Lost Ones*, asked Beckett in 1976 about the accuracy of the statistics specified in the text. Was the flattened cylinder sixteen meters high, as given in the original French version, or eighteen meters high, as printed in the first English edition? Beckett finally settled on sixteen. "After all," he told the actor when they parted on the boulevard Saint-Jacques in Paris, "you can't play fast and loose with pi."

In *The Lost Ones* Beckett experiments with the visual power of words in what is essentially articulated as a vocal medium. Language is a spoken act, even as it is written down, recorded, and read. To be is to be heard. Urging his words "on," the voice is always the hero, in prose just as in Beckett's theater. "Saying," the word the fictional Molloy uses to say it, "is inventing." Beckett's exploration of image, sound, and voice continues in the *Fizzles* (*Foirades* in French), "for to end yet again." *Still*, written in English and first published in *The Malahat Review* in January 1975, condenses the conflict between motion and rest, light and darkness, and sound and silence into one paragraph. The word "still" appears 24 times, here an adverb, here an adjective, here a noun. Shifty and unstable, it is sometimes "silent," sometimes "motionless," sometimes "yet." And *yet* it is always heard: one sound holds all its meanings, moods, and modes. It is a voice, "impossible to follow let alone describe," that makes an "all," a "quite," or a "still." This is a still-life after all.

Beckett told his German translator Elmar Tophoven that he was thinking of *Jeremiah* when he wrote *Company* (1980): "A voice comes to one in the dark. Imagine." The Hebrew prophet was pessimistic about the present and predicted a calamitous future. Beckett's voice isn't quite so sure. Before "the one on his back in the dark" is left unmercifully "alone," the last word in this text, scenes from the past intrude to keep him company in the fictive present. This is a "fable of one fabling of one with you in the dark." It is also, as Beckett's British publisher announced, "his *Wilhelm Meister*." Written in English (though published first in French), *Company* dramatizes the fluidity remembrance imposes on autobiography. Memory calls back vignettes from a life lived long ago in the Irish landscape of Beckett's childhood and shapes them into lies like truth. There are, then, two voices here, the voice of memory and the voice of reason. Beckett gives rapid rhythm to the first and slow rhythm to the second, then lets them play against one another in vigorous counterpoint. The interlocutory nature of this piece has therefore made it an attractive vehicle for theatrical adaptation. In London Stephen Moore starred in John Russell Brown's *Company* for the National Theatre in September 1980, the same year the voice of Patrick Magee

117   David Warrilow in the Mabou Mines adaptation of The Lost Ones, *directed by Lee Breuer with music by Philip Glass (New York, 1972)*

118 *Julian Curry at the Donmar Warehouse (London, 1987) in Katharine Worth's stage adaptation of* Company, *directed by Tim Pigott-Smith*

was heard reading *Company* on BBC Radio 3 in July. Tim Piggott-Smith staged another London version in 1987, starring Julian Curry and produced by Katharine Worth. The show was later seen at the Edinburgh Festival and travelled to New York in April 1988. In America *Company* has also been given two separate stagings. In 1983 Frederick Neumann directed the work with Honora Ferguson for Mabou Mines in New York. "I don't know," the playwright told the director, "what you could do with it. It all takes place in the dark." "That's where theater takes place," Neumann responded, "in the dark." Stan Gontarski's 1985 Los Angeles production with Alan Mandell was the English-language premiere of Pierre Chabert's *Compagnie*, which opened on November 15, 1984 at the Théâtre du Rond-Point in Paris. Beckett, who worked closely with Chabert, advised him to pay special attention to words like *terminé* (concluded), for the accent on the last syllable is also heard as *né* (born). Language recited on a stage has a secondary memory of its own, in this case a desperate matter of life and death.

Beckett followed *Company* with two more stories, *Mal vu mal dit* (1981), written in French, and *Worstward Ho* (1983), in English. His translation of the first, a mine-field of allusion to French and English poetry, appeared in *The New*

119   In 1985 S. E. Gontarski directed Alan Mandell in Company *at the Los Angeles Actors'
Theatre. The production was based on Beckett's stage adaptation for Pierre Chabert's* Compagnie,
which played in Paris the year before.

120   *Beckett in 1973*

121   Right: *Beckett at the bar in the lobby of the Riverside Studios, London*

Yorker on October 5, 1981 as *Ill Seen Ill Said*. Beckett weaves a mysterious fable of a woman who abandons her cabin to seek precarious shelter in the shade of Druidic stones, resembling the cromlech off Brighton Road near Beckett's childhood home in Foxrock. The voice here makes use of a wide theater vocabulary, including "rafters," "boards," and a single "trapdoor." *Julius Caesar*, *Love's Labour's Lost*, *Much Ado About Nothing*, *Hamlet*, *Othello*, *Macbeth*, and *King Lear* provide us with more than enough Shakespeare. John Milton's closet drama, *Samson Agonistes*, is there too. The "curtain closes" on this tale, however, with a nod to Ecclesiastes, "Know happiness," which is also a pun. There can be no happiness in this *Godot*-like "zone of stones," for the voice has its sight on Golgotha, "the place of the skull" (Matthew 27:33).

Worstward Ho, which Beckett has not translated into French, offers us a landscape almost exclusively verbal. There is little appeal here to any world outside of language itself. Every word is nonetheless fated to be the worst word, "said nohow on." Beckett takes his cue from Edgar's aside in *King Lear*, a line he singled out in a notebook he kept in Germany in the 1930s: ". . . the worst is not/So long as we can say, 'This is the worst'." The original sin is syntax itself. Even "said" turns out to be "missaid." Still, "no try no fail." Everything "oozes," a word voiced long ago in the dialogue Beckett wrote for *Endgame*. Language is a universe onto itself: the words presuppose a voice which before long presupposes a man, a woman, and a child. Humanity seems to be starting all over again. In the beginning was the word and that's how it is, apparently, in the end too: "The words too whosesoever. What room for worse! How almost true they sometimes almost ring!" It was precisely this human dimension to verbal abstraction which Frederick Neumann was able to uncover when he adapted *Worstward Ho* for the stage and brought it to New York in 1986. Theater in its manifold forms proved to be, once again, an intensely humanizing force.

When asked in 1985 if *Company*, *Ill Seen Ill Said*, and *Worstward Ho* constituted a trilogy, Beckett said, "I hadn't thought of it as such, but I suppose so—more so than the other works called the Trilogy." The connection between three works is now primarily stylistic and formal as we watch the subject-object relations constantly realigning themselves, but always moving toward one common goal, "a pox on void." "Joyce was a synthesizer," Beckett said. "I am an analyzer." In a post-Pythagorean age, which is just as assuredly post-Christian, the remnants of unity still come in threes. "Look at the world," the tailor says in the famous punch-line to the joke Nagg repeats in *Endgame*, "and look at my TROUSERS!" "I tell this story"— which is always the same story—"worse and worse." In his most recent work in prose, three short pieces he originally called "Fragments," but later changed to "Still Stirrings" and finally *Stirrings Still*, Beckett continues to keep visionary company with words and the voice that cries out for communion with them. "Who knows?" Beckett said about the state of his unfinished writings as late as 1987. "There may still be some more stirrings." By the turn of the new year, 1989, he had completed one more prose piece, this one in French and called, not surprisingly, *Comment dire*. There's a before Beckett, a with Beckett, as there will surely be an after Beckett, yet in each case the shape he gives to the human imagination will never be quite the same again. He leaves, as Harold Pinter said, "no maggot lonely." At close of so long a day, the sun shines out, weary with weariness, if only for a moment a "rude awakening." Before dark comes and threatens to overwhelm us all, readers and listeners, there is, once again, evensong. It is this frail instant of light, "when less did not seem possible," that Beckett urges us to memorialize and celebrate with him. Always "waiting for Godot to come . . . or for night to fall," there's still Beckett, still writing, still "listening for a sound." The whole of Beckett is written into every line: "Said nohow on," but still *On*. "What are you writing at the moment," the director Rocky Greenberg asked Beckett at the Riverside Studios in London in the 1980s. "Another blot on silence."

122   "... I have never in my life been on my way anywhere, but simply on my way."

Bibliography

ACHESON, JAMES, and KATERYNA ARTHUR, eds. *Beckett's Later Fiction and Drama: Texts for Company*. London: Macmillan, 1987.

BAIR, DEIRDRE. *Samuel Beckett: A Biography*. New York: Harcourt, Brace, Jovanovich, 1978.

BEJA, MORRIS, S. E. GONTARSKI and PIERRE ASTIER, eds. *Samuel Beckett: Humanistic Perspectives*. Columbus: Ohio State University Press, 1983.

BLUMENTHAL, EILEEN. *Joseph Chaikin: Exploring at the Boundaries of Theater*. Cambridge: Cambridge University Press, 1984.

BRATER, ENOCH. *Beyond Minimalism: Beckett's Late Style in the Theater*. Oxford and New York: Oxford University Press, 1987.

——, ed. *Beckett at 80/Beckett in Context*. Oxford and New York: Oxford University Press, 1986.

——, ed. *Journal of Modern Literature* 6, 1 (February 1977). Special Beckett number.

CALDER, JOHN, ed. *As No Other Dare Fail*. London: Calder, 1986.

CHABERT, PIERRE, ed. *Revue d'esthétique: Samuel Beckett*. Privat: Paris and Toulouse, 1986.

COHN, RUBY. *Back to Beckett*. Princeton: Princeton University Press, 1973.

——. *Just Play: Beckett's Theater*. Princeton: Princeton University Press, 1980.

——. *From "Desire" to "Godot": Pocket Theater of Postwar Paris*. Berkeley: University of California Press, 1987.

——, ed. *Casebook on "Waiting for Godot"*. New York: Grove Press, 1967. Rev. ed. London: Macmillan, 1987.

ESSLIN, MARTIN, ed. *Samuel Beckett: A Collection of Critical Essays*. Englewood Cliffs, N.J.: Prentice-Hall, 1965.

FINNEY, BRIAN H. *Since "How It Is": A Study of Samuel Beckett's Later Fiction*. London: Covent Garden, 1972.

FLETCHER, BERYL S., and JOHN FLETCHER. *A Student's Guide to the Plays of Samuel Beckett*. Rev. ed. London: Faber & Faber, 1985.

FLETCHER, JOHN. *The Novels of Samuel Beckett*. 2nd ed. London: Chatto and Windus, 1970.

GONTARSKI, S. E. *The Intent of "Undoing" in Samuel Beckett's Dramatic Texts*. Bloomington: Indiana University Press, 1985.

GRAVER, LAWRENCE, and RAYMOND FEDERMAN. *Samuel Beckett: The Critical Heritage*. London: Routledge & Kegan Paul, 1979.

HARVEY, LAWRENCE E. *Samuel Beckett, Poet and Critic*. Princeton: Princeton University Press, 1970.

KALB, JONATHAN. *Beckett in Performance*. Cambridge: Cambridge University Press, 1989.

KENNER, HUGH. *A Reader's Guide to Samuel Beckett*. New York: Farrar, Straus and Giroux; London: Thames and Hudson, 1973.

KNOWLSON, JAMES, ed. *"Happy Days": The Production Notebook of Samuel Beckett*. New York: Grove Press, 1985.

——, ed. *Samuel Beckett's "Krapp's Last Tape": A Theatre Workbook*. London: Brutus Books, 1980.

——, ed. *Samuel Beckett: A Celebration*. Reading: The Beckett Archive, 1986.

——, and JOHN PILLING. *Frescoes of the Skull: The Later Prose and Drama of Samuel Beckett*. London: Calder, 1979.

McMILLAN, DOUGALD and MARTHA FEHSENFELD. *Beckett in the Theatre*. London: John Calder, 1988.

O'BRIEN, EOIN. *The Beckett Country: Samuel Beckett's Ireland*. Dublin: Black Cat Press; London: Faber & Faber, 1986.

O'MÓRDHA, SEAN. *Samuel Beckett: Silence to Silence*. Documentary for Radio Telefis Éireann, 1987.

REILLY, JOHN. *The Beckett Project*. Global Village, New York, 1987–89.

ROBINSON, MICHAEL. *The Long Sonata of the Dead: A Study of Samuel Beckett*. New York: Grove Press, 1969.

SCHLUETER, JUNE, and ENOCH BRATER, eds. *Approaches to Teaching Beckett's "Waiting for Godot"*. New York: MLA Publications, 1989.

SCHNEIDER, ALAN. *Entrances: An American Director's Journey*. New York: Viking Press, 1986.

WORTH, KATHARINE. *The Irish Drama of Europe from Yeats to Beckett*. London: Athlone Press, 1978.

ZILLIACUS, CLAS. *Beckett and Broadcasting*. Abo, Finland: Acta Academiae Aboensis, Ser. A. Humaniora, 51, no. 2, 1976.

Acknowledgments

For their help and guidance in preparing this study, the author would like to thank Ruby Cohn, Linda Ben-Zvi, Martin Esslin, Barry McGovern, John Calder, Martha Fehsenfeld, Benedict Nightingale, Elmar Tophoven, James Knowlson, Lois Overbeck, Frederick Neumann, Rocky Greenberg, Billie Whitelaw, David Warrilow, Pierre Chabert, Kitts Mbedoh, H. Porter Abbott, Barney Rosset, and, of course, Mr. Samuel Beckett, the only true begetter.

Sources of Illustrations

BC refers to illustrations from *The Beckett Country: Samuel Beckett's Ireland* by Eoin O'Brien, published by the Black Cat Press and Faber and Faber, 1986. Numerals refer to illustration numbers.

Berenice Abbott 18, 19; Agence de Presse Bernand 61; Jerry Bauer 1, 120; Courtesy BBC (Enterprises) 1966 103; BBC Hulton Picture Library 13, 14; Photo Cecil Beaton courtesy of Sotheby's, London 23; The Beckett International Foundation, The University of Reading 41, 87; Courtesy Francesca Bion 36; Philippe Charpentier 45; Courtesy Mrs C. Clarke 4 (*BC* p. 40); Nobby Clarke 62, 63; Fred Conrad/The New York Times 65; Courtesy Miss M. Crowley 43 (*BC* p. 329), 44 (*BC* p. 319); David Davison 3 (*BC* p. 6), 7 (*BC* p. 112), 33 (*BC* p. 132), 34 (*BC* p. 134); Zoe Dominic 67, 68, 69, 82, 84, 85, 88, 93, 95; Brigitte Enguerland 106; Marc Enguerand 94, 97, 108; Richard Feldman 76; Gisèle Freund 21; Courtesy Miss J. Gaffney 42 (*BC* p. 325), 44 (*BC* p. 319); S. E. Gontarski 114, 119; Harlingue-Viollet 16, 39, 54; Irene Haupt 107; Harry Ransom Landry 117; Lapi-Viollet 38; Tom Lawlor/Gate Theatre, Dublin 64; Antoni Libera 110; Lipnitzki-Viollet 17, 53, 56, 57, 60, 70, 71, 78, 79, 80, 81, 83, 90, 92; Joe B. Mann 91; Man Ray 31; Meridian 119; John Minihan 40, 51, 89, 116, 121, 122; Courtesy Caroline Murphy 2 (*BC* p. 343), 6 (*BC* p. 14), 37; National Film Archive, London 29, 86, 100; National Gallery of Ireland, Dublin 27; National Library of Ireland, Dublin 10, 11, 12; National Portrait Gallery, London 52; Roger Pic 55; Georges Pierre 66; Portora Royal School, Enniskillen 9; Private Collection 28; Courtesy Barney Rosset 99; Roger Jean Segalat Archive 32; Frank Serjack 101; Courtesy Morris Sinclair and Gottfried Büttner 35; Edwin Smith 8; Amelia Stein/Gate Theatre, Dublin 50; Süddeutscher Rundfunk Stuttgart/Photo Hugo Jehle 104, 111, 112, 113/Photo Christel Korte 102; Martha Swope 75, 96, 105, 109, 115; Yasunari Takahashi 77; Robin Thomas 98; Georges de Vincent 59; Collection Viollet 15; Reg Wilson 73, 74; Katharine Worth 118; Zaiks/Photo Zygmunt Rytka 110.

Sources of Quotations

Extracts from Beckett's works are reproduced by kind permission of Faber & Faber Ltd, London; John Calder Ltd, London; and Grove Press, New York.

Index